"The Amazing Storyteller  great book...*Spiritually Fr*... read and filled with fresh insight for every parent. Parenting can be overwhelming at times. You are asked to be a provider, coach, referee, and teacher. You have to be patient, disciplined and loving. The good news is you don't have to make this incredible adventure alone. Whether you are a first-time parent, or an experienced journeyman, Pastor Terrell's newest book is an excellent partner. He does a masterful job of teaching you helpful principles, giving you practical examples and encouraging you every step of the way. Pastor Terrell's book has been lived out in the real world. I've seen his and Shanda's parenting up close and I can fully recommend this book. It's a book that you will not only want to read but keep on the nightstand to continually reference.

>**Troy Gramling**
>Lead Pastor, Potential Church

When we read any book on parenting advice, sometimes we may wonder if the author really, actually lived out the teaching. Well, having known Pastor Terrell since his children were very young, I can tell you that he has lived out this very practical advice. I have watched his children grow up to live out this wisdom in a very real way. I was able to watch Pastor Terrell teach and live out this wisdom and that influence from him had such a great impact on my own parenting. So, I highly recommend this book! Thank you, Pastor Terrell!

>**Gary Baldus**
>Lead Pastor, New Walk Church

Parenting is a journey filled with both joys and challenges and in *Spiritually Freed Parenting: Raising Future Adults*, Pastor Terrell Somerville provides a much-needed guide for those navigating this sacred responsibility. Rather than focusing solely on the daily struggles of parenting, Somerville urges readers to approach it with the end goal in mind: raising children who grow into passionate, lifelong followers of Jesus. Terrell doesn't just offer abstract encouragement—he lays out a clear, scripture-based blueprint that helps parents stay intentional in their approach. It's all too easy to get lost in the day-to-day grind, but this book serves as both a reminder and a roadmap, helping parents keep their ultimate mission in focus. As a parent, I don't just want my daughters to be obedient for the sake of compliance; I want them to develop a deep, personal faith that shapes their lives. This book reinforces that desire, challenging and equipping me to lead them well.

Dr. Jason Baugh,
Lead Pastor, Center Point Church

"With practical wisdom, real-life humor, and biblical truth, Spiritually Freed Parenting empowers parents to raise confident, resilient, and faith-filled kids. Pastor Terrell offers a refreshing, down-to-earth guide to navigating parenthood while building strong character in the next generation."

Dr. Chris Vaught,
Lead Pastor, Connection Point Church

Spiritually Freed Parenting by Terrell Somerville is a must-read for parents seeking to raise their children with faith, grace, and biblical wisdom. With heartfelt insights and practical guidance, this book equips parents to break free from fear and embrace God's design for their family. Terrell and Shanda's experience and passion shine through every page, offering a roadmap to raising spiritually strong and resilient children. This book will encourage, challenge, and inspire parents to lead their families with confidence and faith. Highly recommended!

Carl Nichols
Lead Pastor, Relevant Church

Spiritually FREED

Parenting

Raising Future Adults

Terrell Somerville

LEAD PASTOR – FREEDOM CHURCH

Dedication

I cannot give honor praise and glory to my Savior Jesus Christ enough for allowing me to serve Him! He has given me the privilege and responsibility to be a Christian, husband, father, Papa T, and pastor.

To my beloved wife, Shanda, who gave me her love, her heart, and her hand in marriage. She is the most incredible Christian, wife, mother, Nana, and pastor's wife that I could have ever dreamed of. To our three amazing daughters, Lily, India, and Chloe who are living out their lives for Jesus being great examples of wives and mothers. And to our 13 wonderful grandchildren. 11 are present and twins on the way; I can't give thanks to God enough for each of you. You all are an incredible joy for Papa T and Nana to love and watch each of you to grow into what God knit you together in your mother's wombs to become!

Copyright © 2025 Terrell Somerville
All rights reserved. No part of this publication may be reproduced, distributed, or transmitted in any form or by any means, including photocopying, recording, or other electronic or mechanical methods, without the prior written permission of the publisher, except in the case of brief quotations embodied in critical reviews and certain other noncommercial uses permitted by copyright law.

ISBN: 979-8-9901918-0-8

Scripture Quotations Notice: Unless otherwise noted, Scripture quotations in this book are taken from the Holy Bible, New Living Translation (NLT), copyright Â© 1996, 2004, 2015 by Tyndale House Foundation, used by permission, all rights reserved, and the Holy Bible, New International Version® (NIV®), copyright Â© 1973, 1978, 1984, 2011 by Biblica, Inc., used by permission, all rights reserved worldwide.

Table of Contents

FOREWORD 11

Introduction: Raising Future Adults, not just Kids 13

Chapter 1 Building a Faith Foundation 23

Chapter 2 Teaching Responsibility and Respect 39

Chapter 3 Developing Emotional Resilience 53

Chapter 4 Giving Godly Discipline 67

Chapter 5 Nurturing a Servant's Heart 83

Chapter 6 Raising Leaders who follow Jesus 97

Chapter 7 Teaching Resilience in Faith 109

Chapter 8 Encouraging a Heart of Gratitude 121

Chapter 9 Biblical Identity & Future Adults 131

Chapter 10 Nurturing a Passion for God's Word 143

Chapter 11 Parenting Prodigal Kids 153

Chapter 12 Parents Passing Christian Heritage 163

Conclusion: Raising Future Adults God's Way 177

Acknowledgements 183

FOREWORD

I could not have written this book. I am not qualified. In order to write a book like this you must live the life and walk the talk. I will explain what I mean by that in this Foreword. In my own book, *In Pursuit of His Glory*, an account of my twenty-five years as the minister of Westminster Chapel, I conclude with a chapter called "If I Could Turn the Clock Back". In this chapter, I explain that if I could turn the clock back, I would put my family first.

We came to England not for me to be the minister of Westminster Chapel but to do a research degree at Oxford University. On the first day with my supervisor, Dr. B. R. White, I received advice I was not expecting from an Oxford don: "Don't forget your family. These days at Oxford will pass quickly. You won't get these years back". But I rationalized my priorities. I wanted to get the degree behind me so that we could return to America, and then I would put my family first. Our son T. R. prayed before every meal, "Thank you God for the food and help daddy to get his D.Phil. so we can go back to America".

Just as I was finishing my work at Oxford, I was invited to preach at Westminster Chapel. They asked me to become their minister. After a few weeks our son came to me, crying,

"Daddy, you said we were going home to America, and we are still here". I could not look at him in the eyes. Twenty-five years later I was asked to do an interview for the Billy Graham Association. I will never forget the interviewer's words, "That's fifty-nine minutes, Dr. Kendall. We have one minute left. Tell us about your family and your role as a father". I immediately replied, "Stop. Don't film. On this I have been a failure. I put the church first. I put sermon preparation first, thinking I was putting God first. I now believe that if I had put my family first, I would have preached just as well, but I cannot get those years back". Enough said.

I recommend Terrell Somerville's book. I wish I had read it fifty years ago. Terrell does not have the degrees I have, but he has the wisdom I did not have. To those who read and apply what Terrell puts in this book, you will be a good parent. You will never be sorry you take the wisdom and advice found in this book. I should also add, it reads well. You will go from laughing to feeling convicted, I promise!

Dr. R. T. Kendall
Minister and Author

Introduction

Raising Future Adults, not just Kids

I will never forget Sunday, August 11th, 1991, around 3:00 in the morning. Shanda was full term in her pregnancy with our first child, Lily. She had gone to the bathroom feeling like she was constipated. I thought to myself, I bet Shanda is not constipated, she is going into labor. I mentioned to her that she may be going into labor, and she gave me a strong rebuke that this isn't labor pain, it was in her back. Then, I decided to start timing her intense times of pressure, and they seemed to be coming on systematically. So, since she was close to her due date, I called her mother Barbara who said, "She's about to have a baby." So, I told Shanda what her mom said, and we quickly got ready to go to the hospital. The three of us loaded up and headed out.

Of course, being a "Soon to be new Dad" I wanted to turn on the flashers to drive Shanda to the hospital. I guess that idea came from the movies. She told me to slow down! She feared my driving anyway. Also, Shanda hates any attention on herself and having the flashers on made her feel dramatic to say the least.

After arriving, they got Shanda checked in. The nurse checked her and said that she was dilated to three and that we should have a baby here by tonight. I said tonight? I was frustrated at her comment because it was still in the very early morning.

Showing my impatience, I pulled my cap down over my eyes and reclined in the chair provided for a "Soon to be new Dad" who was clueless about the laboring process of a first-time mother. The anesthesiologist wasn't in a hurry to leave home when he factored in that this was Shanda's first baby. He took his time showering before heading to the hospital. He shared this with Shanda later in the form of an apology, and here is why.

Shanda's contractions and the dilation quickly progressed. I thought that I would be a great help and coach her on the "How to have a Baby Process." Every time she would have a contraction, the pain was very intense. I proceeded to tell Shanda to watch the clock, concentrating on it instead of the horrible pain she was going through.

After multiple episodes, Shanda's sweet personality made a swift and sharp change due to my coaching on the "How to have a Baby Process". She took the dampened washcloth being used to soothe her forehead and popped me across my head with it. She quickly said, "You get to massaging my feet, and stop trying to tell me how to have a baby." You know what I told her after this fiasco? "Yes Ma'am."

Shanda had quickly gone from a dilation of three to ten, so when the anesthesiologist finally came in the room, he apologized moving swiftly to ease her labor pain with an epidural. It wasn't very long from then that the nurse started telling Shanda to "Push, Push, Push" in quick phrases to get our Lily into her new world. Unfortunately, Lily was stuck in the birthing canal and wasn't moving despite Shanda's efforts. The anesthesiologist pressed on Shanda's belly for the doctor, and thereafter at 10:47 a.m., out popped our icky, red-faced, cone-shaped head, beautiful baby daughter Lily Shantera Somerville. Before they put a hat on her head, Lily looked like the cone heads on "Saturday Night Live" had had a baby. The doctor let us know not to worry, that due to Lily being stuck in the birthing canal, this is why her head was like that. Of course, by the next day, her head was perfectly normal.

Shanda and I were overjoyed as well as our family for this brand-new human coming into our lives. It was so surreal to me that we would now be responsible for this new life God gave us to protect, provide, nurture, and lead into the life God made her to be. After this, we were blessed over the next few years to have two more daughters.

India Alexis Rose, our "tax baby," was born on December 30th, 1994. Chloe Israel, our "surprise baby," was born on October 23rd, 1997. One life lesson I learned from Lily's birth was not to ever coach Shanda on the "How to have a Baby Process." I would advise any" Soon to be new Dad" to learn this life lesson as well.

I'm not sure where the term "Raising Future Adults" came from or I would give credit; however, it's been my heart from the day I first became a parent. This book is not written from a perfect way of parenting because there are no perfect ways or perfect parents. However, Shanda and I together followed as close as possible to God's way of parenting from His Word, our own parent's experience, and a whole lot of prayer. And yes, we are thankful for God's grace through our mistakes and failures as we parented our three girls.

Parenting is one of life's greatest callings—a sacred assignment entrusted to us by God. It's a role filled with both challenges and immeasurable rewards.

Yet, in the middle of extensive daily routines, school drop-offs, soccer practices, beauty pageants, music lessons, birthday parties, meal prep, and bedtime stories, not to mention me putting Chloe's hair up into a ponytail for school which she hated, it's easy to focus on short-term goals. We all want our kids to behave well, get good grades, and stay out of trouble. While these are important, God calls us to something far greater: to prepare our children for a life that honors Him and that our children become what He created them for to fulfill their purpose.

Again, we're not just raising children; we're raising future adults. And more than that, we're raising future disciples of Christ. As parents, our task is not just to guide our children through their formative years but to equip them for a lifetime of walking in faith and freedom. We must always remember that parenting is with eternity in mind. Parenting can become such a short-sighted goal. Through the following pages, my prayer is that you take a 30,000-foot view of what Biblical Parenting is. Whether you are hoping to be a parent, you're in the thick of parenting, an empty nester, a grandparent, or simply around kids, our influence has lasting effects of good or bad.

Also, my prayer is that you will realize how parenting is your opportunity to be used by God to shape them into what will bring Him the most glory. The most formable window is the first 10 years! The world measures parenting success by achievements: academic awards, sports trophies, and financial independence. But as followers of Christ, we're called to measure success differently.

Proverbs 22:6 (NLT) offers timeless wisdom...
"Direct your children onto the right path, and when they are older, they will not leave it."

Giving Godly directions, every day is crucial to get them onto the path where God wants to lead them. You plant seeds of faith through God's Word, God's ways, and through unceasing prayer for and with your children. You have a season of influence when the seeds will be planted. Even if they leave the right path when they become teenagers (when we think an alien has taken over their bodies), those seeds you planted are still there, though they may be dormant for a while. I have also included in this book a chapter on parenting a prodigal child to help those facing this pain. Being in ministry for over 30 years, I have counseled and prayed with many broken-hearted parents over their kids taking a wayward direction.

I had a picture on my wall in my office for many years that said, "Begin with the End in Mind." So, in parenting, as with any endeavor of value to us, "Always begin with the end in mind." The way we nurture, teach, and lead our children today will influence the adults they become tomorrow. Will they grow into individuals who know and trust God? Will they make choices rooted in faith, or will they follow the shifting values of the world that's not on our side? Parenting with eternity in mind shifts our focus from raising children who simply *fit in* to raising children who *stand out* for Christ.

Why Focus on "Future Adults?"

The phrase "future adults" highlights a crucial reality: childhood is temporary, but adulthood is forever. One day, our children will leave our homes and face a world full of challenges, opportunities, and temptations. Our responsibility is to prepare them for that moment—not just academically or socially but most of all spiritually. For Shanda and me, our ultimate goal was that when our daughters leave our home and are faced with many mounting and hard life decisions, they will seek the Lord for answers.

When we see our children as future adults, it changes how we approach parenting. Instead of controlling their behavior, we focus on shaping their hearts. Instead of simply managing today's problems, we instill values and truths that will guide them for a lifetime.

Raising future adults means asking tough but important questions:

- Are we helping our children build an unshakable foundation of faith?

- Do they know how to navigate life with wisdom and integrity?

- Are we modeling the kind of Christlike behavior we want them to emulate?

In *Spiritually FREED Parenting*, everything stems from our relationship with Jesus.

John 8:32 (NLT) "And you will know the truth, and the truth will set you free."

So, when Jesus sets us free through forgiveness of our sins, He then gives us the present power of the Holy Spirit. We follow the Bible as directives for our own lives as well as investing and influencing these gifts of our children to help them become His disciples.

The FREED Framework this book introduces is a biblical framework for raising spiritually strong and independent future adults. FREED represents five essential principles:

1. **F**aith Foundation: Helping your children develop a personal relationship with God that anchors their lives.

2. **R**esponsibility and Respect: Instilling accountability and a Christlike regard for others.

3. **E**motional Resilience: Teaching them how to face life's challenges with courage and faith.

4. **E**ternal Perspective: Guiding them to prioritize God's kingdom over worldly success.

5. **D**iscipleship in Action: Leading by example and equipping them to live out their faith daily.

These principles are rooted in Scripture and designed to help you build a legacy of faith in your family.

The Parenting Journey: Growing Together

Parenting is as much about our growth as it is about our children's. It is a journey that refines, humbles, and strengthens us. There will be days when you feel confident and days when you feel completely inadequate. Trust me, Shanda and I know this from experience! But the good news is this: you don't have to parent alone. God's grace is sufficient, His wisdom is available, and His Spirit is ready to guide you.

Again, this book is not about being a perfect parent, it's about walking with a perfect God. It's about surrendering your parenting to Him and trusting Him with your children's future.

Throughout this book, you will find biblical encouragement, practical tools, and real-life examples to inspire and equip you. Each chapter will focus on a specific aspect of the FREED framework, with actionable steps to help you implement these principles in your daily life. You'll also find prayers, reflection questions, and ideas to build a Christ-centered family culture.

Parenting God's way is not easy, but it's worth it. And parenting is a season in our lives that comes in fast and goes by quickly. Together, let's embrace this high calling to raise Spiritually FREED, God-honoring future adults who will make an eternal impact.

Take a deep breath, trust God with the journey, and let's begin this adventure of parenting with purpose, grace, and faith. If you are ready, let's go!

Shanda holding Lily, our first daughter as "Baby of the Week" for the Tennessean newspaper. Does Shanda's sweet face look like someone who would hit her husband with a washcloth?

Chapter 1

Building a Faith Foundation

Proverbs 22:6 (TPT) "Dedicate your children to God and point them in the way that they should go, and the values they've learned from you will be with them for life."

"Faith is taking the first step even when you don't see the whole staircase." *Dr. Martin Luther King Jr.*

A Firm Foundation is so important because every strong structure begins with a solid foundation. A house built on shaky ground will crumble when storms come, but one built on rock can withstand the harshest weather. The same principle applies to raising children. Faith in God is the unshakable foundation that can sustain your children through life's challenges, uncertainties, and temptations.

As parents, our greatest responsibility is to help our children build their lives on the rock of Jesus Christ. This means nurturing their faith in a way that it becomes their own—not just something they inherit from us but something they actively live out.

Faith is caught *and* taught which is why Shanda and I tried our best to lead by example in our faith walk with Jesus. Faith isn't just taught in Sunday school or children's church; it's caught in the everyday rhythms of life. Children learn to trust God not only through Bible stories and prayers but by watching how we, as parents, live out our faith.

- Do they see us prioritizing time with God?

- Do they hear us pray with sincerity?

- Do we handle difficulties with faith or with fear?

After Shanda and I got married, we would have a daily devotion of time with God together. We would read God's Word from the Bible and pray. Church wasn't something that we took lightly either. We devoted ourselves to our church family serving and giving as we grew with our faith community. When our daughters each came into the world, we knew their faith foundation was up to us through our selfless commitment to them. Building faith in Jesus in their lives starts at home.

This picture was taken in 1997 when our youngest, Chloe, was two weeks old.

We started praying and reading Bible stories to them very early in their lives. Not only was praying with them crucial, but we were praying for their future. We would pray for our daughters to fulfill their purpose for God. We would pray they find a Christian spouse if they chose to get married. We would pray that they grow to love the Lord with all their heart, and we prayed that they would have a long, healthy, prosperous life. We took our daughters to church on the very first Sunday that we brought them home from the hospital. We actually brought all three of our daughters to church placed in the same white wicker basket. Prayer and devotion were our daily personal time with God as an example for our daughters. Before we would carry them to school, we would read God's Word together and then ask what they wanted to pray about? Here are verses of scripture about prayer and reading God's Word:

1 Peter 5:7 (NLT) "Give all your worries and cares to God, for he cares about you."

1 Thessalonians 5:17 (NLT) "Never stop Praying."

John 20:31 (NLT) "But these are written so that you may continue to believe that Jesus is the Messiah, the Son of God, and that by believing in Him you will have life by the power of His name."

So, we wanted our girls to know that praying to God and reading the Bible, which is God's heart to us, is the key for life in Christ. I will never forget the acronym for the BIBLE that I learned many years ago: **Basic-Instructions-Before-Leaving-Earth.**

Yes, there were prayer requests that came from our daughters' hearts and minds that would seem childish, yet innocent. At the age of three, Chloe prayed for several years for a boy named Tony from the first church I pastored. I've often wondered how Tony turned out in life because Chloe had a heart for praying for Tony who had a rough home life living in a marginalized situation. He probably became so significant for the glory of the Lord due to all the prayers that Chloe prayed for him!

I remember distinctively on one occasion that India, our middle daughter, called me out about our time of devotion and prayer that we had each morning. It had been one of those crazy weeks during the infancy stage of starting Freedom Church that we were running at breakneck speed. We hadn't had our morning devotion in a couple of mornings, and India said, "Dad, why aren't we having our prayer and devotion? You don't even love us anymore." She recognized that this valuable priority of ours was missing lately, and it mattered. Wow, dagger to the heart. Once again, building faith in our children's hearts is caught and taught. This rebuke of India's was a prime example of what we were instilling in her heart to build a firm faith foundation.

Our attendance to church was never in question. We never had our daughters to come up to Shanda or I and ask, "Are we going to church today?" All three of our girls knew where our devotion and commitment were when it came to the Lord's church. Yes, there will be times that you miss for sickness, work or vacation. However, even when we were out of town, we were going to church somewhere if possible. Remember, our children will embrace what we embrace and love what we love especially in the first ten years of their lives.

Your actions often speak louder than your words. If you want your children to grow up loving God, they need to see that love reflected in you. Let's look at some practical steps to lay a Faith Foundation.

Make God the center in Your Home!

Create daily rhythms that point your family to God. Having morning devotions and family prayer times will raise the spiritual awareness for building the spiritual DNA for your children. Developing this takes discipline. Starting any new habit usually takes about 21 days to get it ingrained into our lives. Beginning a simple habit like thanking God together before meals is a great place to start. As a family, starting every day with Scripture and ending it with each member sharing something they're thankful for. Don't try to have a long intensive family prayer and devotion, or you'll be tempted to give up. Not only that, but your children will also lose interest if this time together is boring.

Shanda and I wanted this time to be before school, and we would be creative to hold our girls' interest. We would have our devotional times with a length of time around five to ten minutes. We had a time where we would show an age-appropriate, five-minute video. You can focus a key verse or a big idea to learn. Discuss how the devotional applies to their daily lives at school, with friends, or at home.

Encourage them to share ways they have seen God work. Keep a prayer journal with everyone's prayer requests to revisit how prayer was working in those situations. And most of all, we would praise God when those prayer requests were answered. At times, we would play a worship song and sing together giving our praise to the Lord. You can give prizes for memorizing Bible verses. You can use YouTube or a streaming service to play interactive kid's worship songs. RightNow Media is a great resource for devotional times with your children. We have this as a free resource at Freedom Church for our families. Remember, this spiritual investment journey with your family is not a sprint, it's a marathon.

Model a personal relationship with God!

The old saying' "Do as I say, not as I do" will not work with how we parent children. They are always watching! We can say what is important to us; however, our actions will always prove otherwise. Spiritual leadership in our homes through our example of our personal relationship with God cannot be stressed enough. Shanda and I would get up early in the morning before our daughters to have our own quiet time with the Lord to read the Bible and pray. I know there are those who would push back and say, "Why can't I have my devotion with the Lord at night? I'm not a morning person." I get that philosophy, and I understand there are those who are more of a night person than an early morning person. However, let me share with you our example for prayer time from Jesus.

Mark 1:35 (NIV) "Very early in the morning, while it was still dark, Jesus got up, left the house and went off to a solitary place, where he prayed."

Giving our top priority to connect with our Father in heaven before we head out into the day's activities is what I see Jesus' example of. Jesus' early morning prayer highlights the importance He placed on communing with the Father before engaging in the day's demands. It sets an example of putting spiritual priorities first while seeking divine guidance and strength for what lies ahead. We have no idea what we will face in each day. I've often mentioned that person at work who might rub you the wrong way- the one you want to "choke in the name of Jesus." When praying as Jesus did, before you begin your day, you will get strength to act like Jesus, not like you. This is a time to seek solitude when the house is quiet, when otherwise it's filled with chaos and other responsibilities. The early morning hours provided Jesus with solitude and quiet, away from the crowds and distractions. This reflects the need for undisturbed time to connect deeply with God, something that's often harder to find during the busyness of the day.

I remember many times that I would be on my knees in prayer or reading my Bible when I would hear the little pitter patter of those tiny feet coming through our home when one or more of our daughters would wake up. Let your children see you reading your Bible, praying, and that you are relying on God. Also, share with your children how God is working in your life. Instead of hiding your struggles, share ways that you are trusting God to answer a prayer you have been praying when it is appropriate. Tell them how you are praying and trusting God to provide for your family as well as how you are praying for your children to help and guide them.

Teach Biblical Truths Consistently

Never think that it's ever too early to introduce your children to God's Word. Shanda and I would read the Word out loud while our girls were still in their mother's womb. We truly believed that we couldn't start sharing God's Word too soon. I loved how Shanda and I, together and separately, would sing worship songs and speak God's Word and prayers over them, even as infants. Through the power of the Holy Spirit, God touches their souls before and right after they enter the world; and thereafter.

You can never start reading the Word of God to your children too early!

Consistency is the key to sharing God's truth. Yes, there will be times that, like our family did, it was all you could do to get out the door to get them to school. And yes, you may miss a morning; however, get back on track. Be consistent. As I shared earlier in this chapter, using stories, having memory verses, and discussions to make the Bible come alive is how you can keep your kid's interest toward God. Be creative with different age-appropriate Biblical resources for younger children or devotionals for teens.

Celebrate Milestones of Faith

Celebrating special moments of your children's spiritual journey lets them know that you not only love them, but you are so very proud of them. Recognize and celebrate these moments like your child's first prayer. A great way to help them start to pray is at bedtime and mealtime. I know that there are parents who are shy when it comes to praying out loud; however, exemplifying prayer is your opportunity to teach them they are getting to communicate with the God of the universe that spoke their very life into existence. Take it to heart and ask God to help you help them have a regular time of praying. You'll see it gets more comfortable and freer as you do.

When they give their heart to Christ for the very first time, my prayer is that it is you as their parents that lead them to salvation. However, it may happen with them praying at home, at children's church, or somewhere else. Wherever and whenever they give their hearts to Christ, throw a BIG celebration or plan a special supper to commemorate the greatest decision they have made and will ever make.

I want to share with you that the Holy Spirit's conviction for each child's heart to ask Jesus to save them comes at different times. Our oldest daughter, Lily, was nine years old when she gave her heart to Christ. I was preaching at a church on a Sunday night. At the end of the service, Lily happened to be sitting on the last pew in the church, and we could see that she was visibly emotional. We weren't sure why, so we sat down to ask her. She proceeded to tell us she wanted to give her heart to Jesus. I was so overcome with emotion that I asked my pastor friend to lead her in the prayer as we all prayed together.

Our middle daughter, India, was five years old when she came forward on a Sunday night service at the only other church I ever pastored. I had preached on "HELL" of all subjects that this young heart could hear. (And somedays you wonder if they even listen during big adult church at all!) At the invitation, India was seated near the back. She came all the way down that long aisle to say she didn't want to go to hell and wanted to be saved. I guess to be honest, the message had "scared the HELL out of her" because she didn't want to go there.

For India, what she received that night is what I call a "head salvation experience." Yes, at five years old she prayed and was sincere. However, she truly came under the Holy Spirit heart conviction in a car ride back from Missouri at 14 years old and was born again. More details about India's salvation experience are shared in chapter 10. Do not ever hold your children back from wanting to pray to receive Jesus as Lord. Yes, of course, seek the Lord in prayer about their interest and pastoral counsel, but do not discourage their heart of wanting Jesus. After all, it is at least a step toward Him, and only they and God know when salvation has truly come into their heart and soul.

Chloe, our youngest daughter, was five years old when she wanted to ask Jesus into her heart. Freedom Church that we started was still meeting in Hendersonville High School in their theater. It was a Sunday morning. Our family was in our church van pulling the trailer with our portable church equipment. The last couple of days previous, we had been practicing for the drama called Heaven's Gates and Hell's Flames that would start that night.

Chloe proceeded to tell myself and Shanda that she wanted to pray and ask Jesus into her heart. You have to understand, we were driving, and she expressed to pray like "NOW." So, we pulled off the road, and we prayed with Chloe as she asked Jesus into her heart. We all just cried and praised the Lord on the side of the road. Salvation is from the conviction of the Holy Spirit and will come at the age of accountability which varies from child to child. It's not a particular age, but their heart's receptivity to the Holy Spirit's calling.

Your child's very first step of obedience to Christ is to be baptized. This is so important to invite your family, friends, co-workers, and neighbors to witness this spiritual event. Why? Because they not only get to see who the Lord of your child's life is, but it may be the only time you can get certain people you love and care for in the doors of a church. At out church, we share an opportunity to receive Christ every service, and the ones you invite may not know Jesus. At the very least, seeds of the gospel can be planted in their lives. These moments are used to reinforce the significance of your children's spiritual journey.

Connect Faith to Everyday Life

Each day of life together as a family, shows how faith applies to real-life situations. Express to your children about trusting God when they're anxious about a test, forgiving a friend, or being kind to someone in need. When you are driving in the car and you see a rainbow in the sky, share with your children that God is the greatest artist of the universe and how that represents what God said about never flooding the earth again. Those are just a few examples of how you can connect faith to daily life. Here are two verses to encourage you in how to invest faith each day in your children's lives…

Deuteronomy 6:6-7 (NLT) "And you must commit yourselves wholeheartedly to these commands that I am giving you today.

⁷ Repeat them again and again to your children. Talk about them when you are at home and when you are on the road, when you are going to bed and when you are getting up."

These two verses paint a beautiful picture of faith formation woven into the daily rhythms of everyday life. Rather than only having spiritual conversations for devotion time, at church or some other formal setting, teach your children about God in everyday moments. Riding in the car is a great place to have spiritual conversations with your children rather than listening to the radio or watching a device. The silence you choose in these times creates an opportunity to have a heartfelt conversation. When you're at home, the time you spend at dinner, while relaxing, walking, playing together, or when preparing for bedtime, seize these teachable moments by consistently integrating faith into daily life. Being strategic to "impress" God's commands on our children over time with small intentional moments can create a deep spiritual legacy, teaching them that God is present not just on Sunday's but in every aspect of life.

Deuteronomy 6:6-7 challenges us to see this responsibility as both a privilege and a sacred calling, trusting that the seeds we plant will bear fruit in God's perfect timing. There will be times in your parenting journey that you will think you are up against a wall trying to build a faith foundation in your children's lives. The enemy will tell you lies like, "I don't feel spiritually strong enough."

Remember, God does not expect perfection from you. He just wants you to have a heart for Him and try your best to pass it on. Your role is not to have all the answers but to point your children to the One who does. Lean into God's grace and use this journey to deepen your own faith. Shanda and I learned so much in our parenting journey with our daughters for building our own faith. I will tell you that there will be times that your child won't seem interested in God. These will be the times that will try your patience; however, you must stay patient and consistent. Know this, seeds of faith often take time to grow. Building a faith foundation isn't an overnight process. You just continue modeling love and truth, trusting that God is working in their hearts.

Another way the enemy will try his best to steal this precious time and season that God gives you to invest faith in your children's lives is when you say, "We're just too busy right now to prioritize faith in God." The devil is good at making you busy in the short term that turns into long term. Evaluate your family's schedule. Here is a real simple spiritual priority flow for your family's lives- God, family, church, work, hobbies or leisure times. Are there activities you can let go of to make room for what truly matters? Faith is not an "add-on" to life — it is the foundation. The deeper principle is making Jesus the center so that every sphere of life, family relationships, church participation, career pursuits, and recreational activities flow from a heart fully devoted to God. When that happens, each area is lived out for God's glory rather than competing for loyalty.

Your parental goal is to help your children develop a faith that becomes their own. One of the greatest gifts you can give your child is the freedom to develop their own relationship with God their way. While you lay the foundation, they must choose to build on it. Encourage them to ask questions because no question is a dumb question when you don't have the answer. It's okay for them to wrestle with doubts because we all do and discover the truth for themselves. Pray regularly for your child's faith to deepen. Pray for God to reveal Himself to them in a personal way, and He will. Just watch God work!

Reflection Questions:

1. What daily practices can you implement to point your children to God?

2. How can you model faith in your own life more visibly?

3. Are there areas where you need to trust God more and let your children see that trust in action?

A thought to remember...

Building a faith foundation isn't about achieving perfection; it's about faithfully planting seeds that God will grow. As you invest in your child's spiritual life, trust that God through the Holy Spirit is working behind the scenes to shape their hearts and guide their steps. There will be times that you will wonder if your children are growing spiritually due to their actions. As you plant those seeds, they may stay dormant for a while, especially as they grow up. Maybe you have children that have grown up and are not presently living for the Lord. You are wringing your hands and spending time worrying about them. Please spend that time you have been worrying replaced with faith and prayer. Give your prodigal kids to God because He made them for a purpose, on purpose. I have devoted chapter 11 to encourage parents who have prodigal kids.

Chapter 2

Teaching Responsibility and Respect

Colossians 3:20 (NLT) "Children, obey your parents in everything, for this pleases the Lord."

"You cannot escape the responsibility of tomorrow by evading it today." Abraham Lincoln

Building Character for Life

Building character for life is paramount. Responsibility and respect are the cornerstones of a strong character and healthy relationships. Children who learn these values early in life are better equipped to navigate challenges, honor authority, and contribute positively to their communities. One example that seems to be fading away is that we taught our girls to honor their elders. If an adult comes up to our children, whether they are introducing themselves or just saying hello, we taught them to stand up and offer a handshake or hug to show honor and respect. Although they weren't perfect at it, the teaching was there, and the seeds were planted.

In today's culture where entitlement and disrespect are often celebrated, raising children with a sense of accountability and regard for others can feel like swimming upstream. Yet, God's Word provides clear guidance for parents: to teach and model these values with love, patience, and consistency.

Teaching responsibility and respect is about more than following rules. It's about instilling a heart of obedience to God, which becomes the foundation for respecting others and taking responsibility for their actions.

Why Responsibility and Respect Matter

If you wonder why responsibility and respect matter so much, just pay attention to how people act in the world around us! Look at society today and the way you see how not only children, but even adults act out in public. I have been upset in my spirit seeing immature adults act out in disrespect and refuse to take responsibility. I have been embarrassed for parents when I see how their children would act. Then, I thought to myself, "What are they teaching them at home?" Responsibility prepares your children for the day that they are independent from your authority and living on their own. As parents, our job is not to do everything for our children but to teach them how to take ownership of their lives.

Responsibility helps them develop skills, confidence, and the ability to handle life's demands. We taught our daughters that they had to do their share of responsibilities in our household. They had to clean their rooms, help with cleaning the house, and pick up after themselves; the list went on. If we don't teach these responsibilities while they are young, then how will they take care of their own households? Once again, we are to prepare them for the next season of their life when we aren't there to coach them along, not to mention being tempted to do things for them. Did we have times that our daughters would give us push back from their daily duties? Yes of course, and it was oftentimes a struggle. However, you cannot allow them to procrastinate, or they will see that they can get away with not doing what they are responsible for. Again, we are preparing future adults, and as parents, we will be doing them an injustice not to hold their feet to the fire, so to speak, to do what we are asking of them.

Respect Builds Healthy Relationships

Teaching our children to have respect builds healthy relationships, not just for their family but in all the relationships that they will develop. Respect for authority, their peers, and themselves allow children to form strong, Christlike relationships. It teaches them to value others as image-bearers of God. For example, whenever our daughters were rude or disrespectful to their siblings, their mother would instruct them to apologize to one another. She would then require they hug one another in love before the strong rebuke of their unbecoming behavior was over. They hated having to stand there hugging each other. Trust me, you could see it in their eyes and posture as if they were hugging a maggot! However, after a few minutes of required hugging, they would end up giggling, and joy would spring up! Smiles would bloom over the dirty part of their former actions. It was a great way of demonstrating how we can turn our frustrations and anger toward another person into joy and thanksgiving quickly with just an embrace and a changed, softened heart.

Our daughters realized through this process that they were wrong to treat their sibling this way, and it was a great way to show that disrespect would not be tolerated. So, after this, Shanda would make them tell one another three things they loved about their sister which was a real challenge because their feelings were struggling to love. She also had them recite Colossians 3:20, "Children, obey your parents in all things, for this is well pleasing to the Lord," out loud to her. If it was recited with any hint of wrong attitude, then they would have to start all over. Let me tell you, they would have a spirit of disdain in the moment, but to this day, our daughters can still quote this verse.

Practical Ways to teach Responsibility

Many of us have grown up in homes where we had our fair share of things to do around the house. Being creative, fair, and systematic in practical ways to teach responsibility takes effort and time. It will be important to assign children age-appropriate tasks. Give them tasks that match their developmental stage, such as picking up toys, doing laundry, dusting the furniture, cleaning the floors, taking out trash, or helping in the kitchen preparing meals. A 5-year-old can help set the table, dust the baseboards with socks on their hands, and many other things while a teenager can be responsible for learning how to budget their money that they earn, take out the trash, or mow the lawn. You can teach them responsibility with almost any duty.

One thing that is crucial is to always establish clear expectations. Be specific about what you expect and explain the importance of their responsibilities. Please understand that they are going to make mistakes, and you must take the time to teach them. It is easy to get frustrated with them and just decide to do it yourself, whatever the task may be. Remember, if you do this, you are doing them an injustice. They will make a mess, and they will not do it like you want, especially the first few times. However, keep in mind to let them try and fail. It is the end game of teaching them how and teaching them why! Instead of saying, "Clean your room." You need to clarify, "Make your bed, put away your toys, and hang up your clothes."

Allow natural consequences when your children do not do what you have clearly outlined for them. Let your children experience the outcomes of their actions (or inactions) when it is appropriate. For instance, if they forget to complete their homework, let them face the teacher's response rather than rescuing them. Don't be a lifeguard parent (I will expound more on this in chapter four) always rescuing them from the consequences that they will face from not doing what they are told when it comes to their responsibilities. Of course, you may help them out the first time they fail to complete a task; however, helping them every time will not teach them as they go along. When they report they have finished a task, go back with them to review their work effort and offer encouragement with any needed insights for next time.

We must give our children the gift, and I said *gift*, of facing the consequences of inaction, procrastination, or even bad decisions. Be sure to give them praise for their effort, not for perfection. Celebrate their progress and encourage them when they struggle. If you want them to excel in their future responsibilities, it will be through encouraging them, not through just focusing on what they did wrong. Raising your voice and fussing at them for what they failed to do won't work; trust me, I have tried it. Encouragement will go a long way when you say something like, "I love how you took care of that without being asked.", "That shows real maturity.", or, "I am so proud of you!" Take every opportunity that you can to encourage, encourage, and encourage your children again and again. They will not get a lot of that from the world we live in. And through experience, we believe you get better results from being a cheerleading parent with occasional and timely discipline than by being fussy too often.

Practical Ways to teach Respect

Aretha Franklin recorded the song, "Respect" in 1967. You may or may not have been alive at the release, but maybe you have heard this song. The song lyrics depict that they want respect when their significant other gets home. We all need to give respect not just at home but in life, especially to one another, so our children can witness this.

Here are some practical ways to teach respect. It begins with modeling respect in your own behavior. Your children will learn how to treat others by observing how you treat them, your spouse, and those around you. Shanda and I made our share of mistakes in this area, and one example is when we would find ourselves in intense fellowship (aka arguing) with one another in front of our daughters. That is when we would humble ourselves, which may have taken some time as we wrestled between flesh and the Holy Spirit, to apologize to each other. Then, we would apologize to our daughters for acting in such a way.

Showing respect with humility is really important for your children to see in you. It's also amazing to me how we can act in any disrespectful way, arguing or being unkind to anyone, then the phone rings and you answer, "Hello, well how are you?", and reply "We are doing great!" Liar, liar, pants on fire! We suddenly shift from being in the boxing ring of an argument to being the happiest-go-lucky person that ever was. I guess that is our human nature, but honestly, if we are truthful, we all have probably done that. Shanda describes this type of response as being fair to the unaware person calling, that we do not burden them with our own frustrations.

Treating people with kindness in the public sector such as in a restaurant or in a place of business is an important example to our children. I have witnessed so many episodes of people being down-right ugly to someone just simply trying to do their job. I'll have to admit, I did the same thing in my early days. Even if someone is disrespectful to us, it does not mean that we are to give disrespect in return. If someone is disrespectful to us, especially when it happens in front of our children, that isn't a license to be disrespectful back. Instead, this is an opportunity for us to teach our children the golden rule. Show them what Jesus said…

Matthew 7:12 (NLT) "Do to others whatever you would like for them to do to you. This is the essence of all that is taught in the law and the prophets."

We need to show patience with someone who is difficult to deal with. We do not have any idea what is going on in someone's life when they are disrespectful or even downright rude. Showing them respect when they have shown you disrespect is a way to plant seeds of God's way in loving, relational interaction. This is also a time to teach our children that we need to pray for people that act in any unwanted way.

How many times do we allow someone who cuts us off in traffic make us so upset that we are tempted, or even follow through, with waving our middle finger at them? Not good, especially if you have your children in the vehicle with you! I learned a valuable lesson about this when Shanda and I were dating. We had just proceeded to get on the interstate after eating at her favorite restaurant. If you are wondering, it was Rafferty's in Bowling Green, Kentucky. She absolutely loves their chicken fingers. Anyway, a car was on our tail very, very close. Mistake number one was me tapping my brakes.

Mistake number two is when they came around me, I rolled down my window and waved with my middle finger. The car was a big Lincoln Town Car. They proceeded to get in front of us hitting their brakes to the point that they slid their car sideways on the interstate to make us pull over. With our hearts pounding, I diverted around them and went as fast as I could to get away. To this day, the thought of flipping a bird haunts me to say the least.

Parents, please understand that we have to teach our children the Biblical basis for respect. Help your children understand that respect honors God. Show them another couple verses of scripture like…

Philippians 2:3-4 (NLT) "Don't be selfish; don't try to impress others. Be humble, thinking of others as better than yourselves. 4 Don't look out only for your own interests, but take an interest in others, too."

One thing you must do in parenting is to correct disrespect firmly and lovingly. When disrespect occurs, address it immediately and explain why it's unacceptable. Provide them an opportunity to make amends. If your child speaks rudely, have them apologize and teach them how to practice phrasing their words respectfully. Above all, in this digital age where parents are giving cell phones to their children at very early ages, don't let them try to text apologies.

We taught our daughters how to have a face-to-face conversation, especially with something like giving a proper apology. Have your child look the other person in the eye and own their transgression. Apologizing to them and to God. It is the right thing to do. The more you teach honor and respect as well as what you will not tolerate, the more they will understand your expectations when they show disrespect to anyone.

Encourage your children to have empathy. This is vital because the last thing we want is for others to look at them and say, "They do not care about anyone but themselves." The essence of following Jesus is to grow in becoming others-centered, not self-centered. Teach your children to consider how their actions and words affect others. When a situation occurs, be sure to have a conversation and ask them, "How do you think your words made your friend feel?" "How do you think being rude to your brother makes them feel?" As parents, we shouldn't miss teachable moment that God affords us to help shape and mold our children's hearts to be like Jesus and not like the world we live in. As the song "Respect" says, "R-E-S-P-E-C-T, find out what it means to me," you not only want your children to find out what it means to you as their parent but also modeling this behavior because it is Godly behavior.

The Role of Discipline in Responsibility and Respect

Discipline plays a critical role in teaching responsibility and respect, but it must be grounded in love and purpose. Effective discipline isn't about punishment; it's about correction and growth. I will expound in more detail about Godly discipline in chapter four. Setting consistent boundaries for your children helps them know the expectations in how their response should be with responsibility and respect. They will thrive when they know the boundaries and consequences of crossing them.

The key is consistency, so they understand that rules are there for their benefit.

Remember, taking the time upfront to explain the "Why" behind the rules will be to their long-term benefit. How many times have we, as we were growing up as well as our children, asked parents the one-word sentence in response to the parental directive, "Why?" This response will often perturb you, and you will be tempted to respond, "Because I said so." Yes, they need to obey; however, this is a great opportunity to share the "Why" to the "What."

Help your children understand that rules aren't arbitrary, they are there to protect them and help them grow in their responsibility and respect. In this digital age of having smart phones, tablets, and streaming on all of them including our TVs, I see how children will challenge their directives when these devices are, to say the least, really addictive. How often do you follow through when you say,

"We turn off the TV during dinner because family time is important to God and to us." Or maybe, "There will be no cell phones being looked at or used in any way while we are having this nice meal at our favorite restaurant."

How many times are we all guilty of grabbing our cell phones out of our pockets or purses to look at social media, emails, or what you are thinking about other than those you love right in front of you? Google says that the average American spend about four hours and thirty-seven minutes per day on their phones. These devices are a constant time stealer from our lives, especially when we are gathered with our family. Set rules in place that will give you more quality time together.

I was shocked a while back in a restaurant when I saw a parent slap their child on the face. I do not know what the reason was, nor was it any of my business; However, doing that isn't the way to bring a heart of correction to your child. When your children mess up and do things that upset you because, in your mind, you know they knew better; that is a teachable moment. Take the time to discipline them privately and respectfully. If you will think back, there has probably been a time in your upbringing or even in your adult life when you were reprimanded in front of your family or in a public way, and that hurts to the core. So, correct your children in a way that upholds their dignity. Avoid public shaming or saying harsh words that demean them. Remember how you may have felt, and you will want to spare your children those feelings as well.

Don't lean too hard one way or the other when it comes to correcting your children. Balancing grace and truth are crucial for building trust, instilling discipline, and nurturing their character. Try to keep the mindset that correction is an act of love, not just punishment. Calmly, and I said *calmly*, explain what they did, and then how and why it was wrong. Trust me, this will go a long way for the future. They will repeat what you said in coming times of correction. They will confess, "I know, Mom" or "I know, Dad".

Again, teaching responsibility and respect requires balancing grace and truth, just as Jesus did in His relationships. Grace means giving your children room to make mistakes and grow without fear of condemnation. Truth means holding them accountable and guiding them toward better choices. Being consistent is key to your children's growth in every area of parenting them. Counting numbers to your children after a situation of bad behavior has taken place such as, "one, two, two-and-a-half, three, three-and-a-half" is procrastination parenting. I know from experience that parenting is hard, you get tired at times saying the same things repeatedly. I know because I have done the same thing. Try to change your parenting mentality to not procrastinate on disciplining your child's behavior. It is hard work up front but will pay off in the long run. You can create an environment where children feel loved and supported while also being challenged to grow.

Reflection Questions:

1. Are you modeling responsibility and respect in your own actions?

2. What tasks or responsibilities could you delegate to your children to help them grow?

3. How do you currently handle disrespect, and how might you approach it differently with a Christ-centered mindset?

A thought to remember…

Responsibility and respect are not just about good behavior; they're about shaping the heart. When we teach our children to be accountable and to honor others, we prepare them to live as Christlike future adults who reflect His love and truth in everything they do. Don't give up and don't give in. Keep in your mind that this season of parenting is really a short one. You too, like myself, will look back eventually and say, "Where did the time go?" You really will.

To be forthwith, Shanda says I became much softer on Chloe than I was on India & Lily.

Chapter 3

Developing Emotional Resilience

John 16:33 (NLT) "I have told you all this so that you may have peace in me. Here on earth you will have many trials and sorrows. But take heart, because I have overcome the world."

"Hardships often prepare ordinary people for an extraordinary destiny." C.S. Lewis

Emotional resilience matters because this life is full of challenges, disappointments, setbacks, and unexpected storms. Emotional resilience is what God can give us as an ability to navigate those difficulties with strength, faith, and hope. For children, this skill doesn't develop automatically; it's cultivated through intentional parenting and by anchoring their identity in Christ.

All three of our daughters are different in how they navigate through the tough times they face in life, especially when they were growing up. We tried our best to help them understand that it isn't how you fall, but it is how you get back up. We are going to face setbacks, however, and teaching our children that those setbacks may be how God is teaching and preparing us for the amazing future for which He created us.

Our three daughters in 2003 at Hendersonville High School where Freedom Church met for four and half years.

In a world that often promotes instant gratification and avoids discomfort, teaching your children how to handle adversity is a gift that will serve them for a lifetime. When rooted in God's Word, resilience becomes more than just emotional strength; it becomes spiritual confidence in God's sovereignty.

Our oldest daughter, Lily, faced her emotional challenges when she went to middle school. She had a lack of self-confidence and that is where we had to help her, as her parents, by knowing that her confidence had to be in who God made her to be. She had friends who would turn on her, stab her in the back, and be mean to say the least. You could call it emotional bullying because they never put their hands on her, but their words of insults and manipulation were like daggers to the heart. It took a long time to help Lily see who she was in Christ. Whenever we put our eyes on people and take our eyes off God that will take us in an unhealthy emotional direction.

The "Christian Recorder" publication of the African Methodist Episcopal Church published the following quote on March 22, 1862, "Sticks and stones may break my bones, but words can never hurt me." I'm sorry to say that this is definitely not the truth. When we would read the hurtful letters written to Lily, we watched her often cry from the words expressed that caused her pain. Lily became confident despite the struggles she faced, but all due to reminding and drilling into her heart of who she was in God and who He created her to be.

Our middle daughter, India, came with a little more experience as she had watched her older sister get hurt time and time again. She was on a learning curve from what Lily was going through in the middle school years. India is a tough, resilient girl with a tender heart. She rose to the occasion not allowing her peers to hurt her the way that Lily experienced. Shanda and I often thought that India wasn't going to get bullied because we had to tell her to stop arm wrestling the boys, and winning against them, since arm-wrestling wasn't very lady-like. However, India did have her share of emotional drama being bullied in high school. However, she had learned to let it go and not respond. As I have often heard the quote and recited it, "Talk to the hand because the face doesn't understand."

Our youngest daughter, Chloe, learned so much from watching the drama that often took place with her older sisters. She developed a calm, collective spirit about her to watch who she would even allow into her friendship world. She really began to get on her sister's nerves by trying to boss them around with such a spirit of confidence. Chloe got fed up with what she witnessed in middle school. She came home one day while she was in the eighth grade disgusted and somewhat emotional. She proceeded to tell her mother and I that she wanted to leave school and be homeschooled. This was an idea she had brought up, as an option from time-to-time, since kindergarten. Yet she was firm this time, and it took Shanda and I by surprise. Chloe told us about the environment of sexually active peers and bad language that was emotionally disturbing to her. She definitely had our full attention.

Chloe went on, while sobbing, to inform us that she had tried to tell her friends what they were doing was a mistake, but they wouldn't listen. Her spirit was grieved even in that moment for them, and her heart just couldn't take that they were choosing to knowingly sin. We told her that moving from public school to home school was a big life-change move. Shanda wanted Chloe to realize the gravity of her request and to not grow fickle by trying to change her mind back and forth. She told Chloe that we would consider it, but she had to write us a letter of why she wanted to be home schooled. This letter would serve as a reminder about this point-in-time that Chloe could refer back to when she faced any emotions or regret about this idea in the future. We slept on it, and the next morning, Chloe was just as adamant about her decision.
Shanda led her through the process of signing up with a homeschool academy to register with and then drove her to

the middle school in order to meet with the principal to withdraw and clean out her locker. Shanda observed Chloe throughout the process to sense whether Chloe had reservations or confusion about it. That never happened. She faced those friends in the hallway during the class exchange while she cleaned out her locker. They cried and hugged each other asking her not to do this. She never wavered. She was so eager, ready to do her part and be responsible, a blessing and help at church. She graduated from high school one year early.

What Does Emotional Resilience Look Like?

A resilient child is not one who never struggles or gets upset but one who learns to process emotions in healthy ways. We taught our daughters to always talk to us. We tried our best to keep an open line of communication with them no matter what they were facing. Clint Eastwood's character Sergeant Thomas Highway in the movie "Heartbreak Ridge" popularized the phrase, "Improvise, adapt, overcome." So, we taught our daughters to face these challenges with this kind of attitude by navigating this life with a positive outlook. The strength came from us as a family seeking God's wisdom and comfort in times of need. We all faced different challenges as a family, but we knew our great God was on the throne. Through Christ, no matter what any of us would face, we would persevere through difficulties without losing hope. Building resilience equips children to face the ups and downs of life without being overwhelmed or defeated.

Practical Ways to Build Emotional Resilience

Teaching our children to trust God in hard times can be a daunting task to say the least. When your child looks at you with tears in their eyes because of a broken heart from their first break up of puppy love, not making the cheer squad or football team, or when you have to relocate to another city for your company so they are now faced with leaving family and friends, it may seem trivial to us as adults. However, in our children's world, it is their world.

I will never forget the day our family pet, our AKC registered sable and white female Collie dog (for those who remember what Lassie looks like) named Belle Beauty, left this world for Heaven. You know all dogs go to Heaven, right? We gave Lily, our oldest daughter, Belle Beauty for Christmas at the age of two. She was named after the Disney movie character in "Beauty and the Beast." Lily still loves that movie to this day. Belle had grown up with our family and had several litters of beautiful Collie pups. Belle had now reached the age of twelve which is about the life expectancy of Collies. I knew that that day would come so I had already got us another male Collie. We named him Rhett Butler because "He was a lover, not a fighter." So, Rhett was a larger pup when the day came that I dreaded.

It was a pretty morning when I looked outside, and I saw Belle Beauty laying on the ground out in front of our storage building behind our house. Lily was in high school, India was in middle school, and Chloe was in grade school. I was backing out of our driveway when Chloe noticed Belle laying under the tree so still and not getting up to come to us. I quickly ran over to where Belle was lying. I knew immediately that she was in bad shape. Her eyes were open, and she appeared to be hanging on to life. I must have told Chloe that Belle was dying because she screamed in agony so loudly. This alerted Shanda and our other two daughters from inside the house, and they ran out to where Belle was.

We all circled around Belle as a family. She looked up seeing each of us individually and that we were all surrounding her. Then, she stretched her mouth open wide, breathing her last breath of life. Time stood still as we absorbed and poured out our grief for her together. A love we had shared for so many years.

This was a hard time for us. Our girls were so broken-hearted, and we didn't make them go to school. This was a crucial time for us to help them understand that times like this will come, that life is about change, and how not many things stay the same. We need to make the most of the time we have as we aren't promised the next moment. It is so healthy as a family together to teach your children this because they must understand that struggles are part of life, but God is always present and faithful. Each moment in life, whether joys or sorrows, is an opportunity to lead your children in the right direction. Show them how to process situations by trusting and loving God through it all. To realize things in life will happen that cause us great pain, but no matter what, we still love the Lord. Those seasons of hardship will pass, and things won't always be the way they may feel right now.

Don't miss times of heartache like we faced with a lost pet, or worse, when you have a loved one leave the world that is close to you and your children to remind them the promises in God's Word like...

Romans 8:28 (NLT) "And we know that God causes everything to work together for the good of those who love God and are called according to his purpose for them."

The Apostle Paul isn't saying that bad things are good, but this verse teaches us that God can use the bad things that happen in our lives to work together for good. Be sure to encourage your kids that it is ok to express their emotions. Let your children know it's okay to feel sad, frustrated, even angry and cry. I know throughout my life in ministry that I have had countless people tell me that they were taught not to cry growing up. They were to suck it up, be strong, and not cry. Wow, what a terrible thing to teach our children when we serve a God who made us in His image, an emotional God that gave us his emotional demeanor.

I have always said that God gave us our tear ducts to be used as rivers to stop heads from swelling up with pride and burst. Teach them to express these emotions in constructive ways. Help them to understand that it is okay not to be okay, but it is not okay to stay that way. "It's okay to feel upset about losing the game. Let's talk about it and pray together for peace."

As parents, we are to model resilience to our children. They will learn how to handle adversity by watching you. You can demonstrate to them that we are in this life and in this family together no matter what we face. Demonstrate how to face difficulties with faith and a positive attitude regardless of the situation. If you're facing a tough situation at work, share age-appropriate details about how you're trusting God to guide you. Ask them to pray for you and with you about your struggles, not just theirs.

Teach your children to not look at any problem they face with a hopeless spirit of defeat but to say, "This isn't a problem, this is an opportunity." This isn't to demean anything happening, especially if it is in any way serious or even hurtful, but to look for ways to solve what has taken place. God has given us skills, and He has given us wisdom through the leadership of the Holy Spirit and His Word.

Encourage your children to think through solutions rather than giving up when challenges arise. If your child is struggling with a school project, help them break it into smaller steps and tackle each one. Be sure to celebrate their perseverance through what they are facing. Remember, encouragement goes a long way in attitude and action. Highlight the value of their persistence, even when outcomes aren't perfect. Praise your child for their effort in learning a new skill, even if they didn't succeed right away. A theme of the New Testament is faith, hope and love. Shouldn't that be our family theme, too? Enduring faith, love, and bright hope for our children for today and tomorrow.

Faith as the Anchor of Resilience

While emotional strength is important, the true source of resilience is faith in God. Remind your children that their ultimate hope is not in their own abilities but in the Lord. What so many Christians can be guilty of is taking for granted the powerful avenue of prayer. Just think, we get to talk to the ruler and creator of the universe. The very God who spoke this world into existence, my life and yours. Teaching our children to depend on prayer in every area of their lives is crucial to what they will face when they

leave our homes. Teach them to pray through their problems.
Let this verse help your perspective about prayer...

Hebrews 4:16 (NLT) "So let us come boldly to the throne of our gracious God. There we will receive his mercy, and we will find grace to help us when we need it most."

We get to come boldly to God's throne not that we are anything, but that God is everything. You get to receive His Mercy, His Grace, and help when you need it the most! It doesn't get any better than that! Prayer gives children a way to bring their worries and fears to God. If your child is nervous about a test, tell them to pray for peace and confidence. Pray with them and for them. Point them to scripture for encouragement teaching your children to find comfort and strength in God's Word.

Here are other verses we taught our daughters to remember when they were facing any kind of difficult circumstance...

Philippians 4:13 (NLT) "For I can do everything through Christ who gives me strength."

Psalm 28:7 (NLT) "The Lord is my strength and shield; I trust Him with all my heart. He helps me, and my heart is filled with joy. I burst out in songs of thanksgiving."

Encourage your children to have a heart of gratitude. I will take a deeper dive into this subject in chapter eight. But a quick point to include now is the importance of understanding that gratitude shifts the focus from problems to God's blessings. Teach your children to thank God, even in their difficult times. I know this will be hard for them to understand; however, we must let them know that we praise God in all things no matter what they are because He is good! You can start a family gratitude journal where everyone writes down one thing they're thankful for each day.

Helping Children Face Life's Storms

Disappointments will always be inevitable. Teach them that failure or rejection is not the end but an opportunity to learn and grow. If your child doesn't make the team, talk about how God might have other plans for them. Better plans, it's true! Loss and grief will happen. However, you have direct insight and life experience to help them process the loss of a loved one, pet, or even a missed opportunity. Encourage them to share their feelings and remind them of God's comfort. Make teachable moments count.

Peer pressure and bullying is a part of being in the human race of growing up around others. Equip your children with the confidence to stand firm in their identity in Christ. Remind them that they are fearfully and wonderfully made (Psalm 139:14).

The Role of Parents in Building Resilience

Let your children know that you will always be there and provide a safe and loving environment that they can depend upon. Children who feel secure in their parents' love are better equipped to handle challenges.

As parents, you balance support while helping them to develop their own independence. While it's important to guide your children, allow them to make mistakes and learn from them. Keep in mind, overprotection can hinder their growth. Encouraging your children with healthy ways of coping through everything you are able to will be key. Teach your children how to manage stress through prayer, exercise, creativity, or talking with you because they can trust you.

Reflection Questions:

1. How do you currently help your children process their emotions?

2. Are there ways you can better model resilience in your own life?

3. What Scripture or prayers can you incorporate into your family's routine to encourage emotional resilience?

A thought to remember...

Resilience is not about avoiding life's storms but learning to stand strong in the midst of them. By teaching your children to trust God, process emotions, and persevere with faith, you equip them with the tools they need to face life with courage and confidence. In this life you will so often have obstacles and problems. You are either coming out of a problem, you are in the middle of a problem, or a problem is headed your way. That, along with some welcome joys, is life! However, with the strength of our relationship in Christ and being there for each other in our families, that is how we overcome!

A family picture in 2007 with our Collie, Belle Beauty.

Chapter 4

Giving Godly Discipline

Proverbs 19:18 (NLT) "Discipline your children while there is hope. Otherwise, you will ruin their lives."

Hebrews 12:11 (NLT) "No discipline is enjoyable while it is happening – it's painful! But afterward there will be a peaceful harvest of right living for those who are trained in this way."

When I was growing up, I didn't see discipline as a form of love. I would guess that when you were disciplined that you didn't see it as a form of love either. I grew up in a home where you got a whipping for disobedience. I would also assure you that there would be those in today's society that would say that I wasn't disciplined, but instead, say that I was abused. When I would do something bad and get into trouble, it was a whipping for sure. My father would take half of an oak tobacco stick, and he would soar that thing across my butt about three or four times. The pain was intense. I am thankful that one of my father's whippings would last me several months.

Did this type of punishment help me behave better and be a more obedient child? Absolutely! The pain of that whipping got my attention, and I didn't want to be disciplined like that any time soon. There are those who say the phrase, "Spare the rod, spoil the child." People use this term in reference to mean that children need discipline to help them grow up into responsible adults. In other words, not become a "Spoiled Brat." Also, many will accredit this to be what the Bible says. That phrase is not a verse in the Bible, but it can be derived from the following verse in Proverbs…

Proverbs 13:24 (NLT) "Those who spare the rod of discipline hate their children. Those who love their children care enough to discipline them."

The point is that when it comes to disciplining your child for bad behavior, (whatever form of punishment as a parent that you decide) you cannot overlook punishing them. If you do, the child will not learn what is right and wrong and become spoiled.

My father was "Old School." He grew up in a home where he got disciplined with a large switch by his father for correcting any disobedience. My grandfather and my father must have read in the Bible the following verses at some point in their lives due to their style of disciplinary punishment…

Proverbs 23:13-14 (NLT) "Don't fail to discipline your children. The rod of punishment won't kill them.[14] Physical discipline may well save them from death."

When we had our own children, Shanda and I found that we didn't want to fail at disciplining our daughters. There were different kinds of punishment. However, we chose to give them a whipping for their worst crimes of disobedience. Shanda and I knew that it did not kill us when our parents would whip us, and I truly believe those whippings from my father did save me. Actually, I will admit, I should have been given many more whippings that

I would have solely deserved. I know this type of punishment isn't for every child, so I will elaborate on types of punishment later in this chapter.

My father told our family many stories of the things that he and his twin brother did wrong to get punished with a whipping. I guess you could say they were somewhat mean. Maybe being my father's son when I was growing up is why I got the nickname, "Terrible Terrell." However, the pain of a whipping is how my grandfather got my father's attention, and the pain of a whipping is how my father got my attention. You can tell a child repeatedly not to touch a hot stove, however, with the allure of curiosity, they end up touching the stove. When they do, the pain sears into their mind and is a reminder not to ever do that again.

This chapter on "Giving Godly Discipline" is not about me telling you what form of punishment you should use to correct your child's bad behavior. This chapter is to help you understand that all corrective measures of discipline is to always be motivated by love for your children. In today's world, discipline is often misunderstood. It is sometimes seen as punishment or an outdated method of parenting. However, in God's design, discipline is an expression of love and guidance. Just as God disciplines those He loves (Proverbs 3:12), parents are called to lovingly correct their children to shape their character and prepare them to walk in righteousness.

Godly discipline is not about control or anger; it's about teaching, guiding, and setting boundaries that reflect God's principles. When done correctly, discipline helps children understand the difference between right and wrong while leading them toward a life of obedience to God. Remember, discipline is not something that you do to your children, it is what you do for your children. However, there are parents who knowingly or ignorantly are undisciplined parents. You may see some of the following characteristics in your own parenting.

Lifeguard Parenting is when you are rescuing your children from consequences. They get into trouble at school, they failed to take their lunch you fixed for them, or worse this pattern continues into their college years. They get a speeding ticket, and you pay it for them. You are not allowing your kids to face their own consequences. This is doing your children an incredible injustice. You may ask why? Check out this verse…

Galatians 6:7 (NLT) "Don't be misled – you cannot mock the justice of God. You will always harvest what you plant."

God has set up our world with a system of consequences. If we all live according to God's Word, there will be blessings. If we live outside the parameters of God's Word, there will be consequences. When it comes to being a lifeguard parent, if we are honest, we have all done this before in some situations. However, it will not be good for our children's long-term responsibility.

Inconsistent Parenting is where we will decide certain boundaries, then we change our minds depending upon the situation. Consistency is key and it leads to reliability. Many parents will decide what the lines and boundaries are in their homes for parenting their children, then one day change them. There is not anything wrong with making parental changes; however, the children will be confused. As parents, we are to draw up the boundaries, explain them to our children, and then go by them. Children will test those boundary lines, but they really do want boundaries, too!

A great example is when one of my daughters would get into trouble. I would tell them when they got home to go to their room because they were going to be disciplined for their actions. They would sometimes fall asleep on the car ride home if we were out and about. I would have to wake them up and follow through with their discipline. You may think this is cruel; however, it is called being consistent in what I would say as their father. Teaching them they could depend on what I said by making sure I kept my words. As I was getting older, I admit I was getting softer about disciplining Chloe, our youngest daughter. When I would think of not following through with discipling her for something, Shanda would call me out on it. Take these next two verses into your heart…

Proverbs 29:15,17 (NLT) To discipline a child produces wisdom, but a mother is disgraced by an undisciplined child. [17] Discipline your children, and they will give you peace of mind and will make your heart glad."

Since you are reading this book, what I believe about you is that you want your children to be wise and to have peace of mind and a glad heart. I do not know if you realize it, but your children will get their concept of God from you. It will be in how you are consistent. It will be in how you treat them. It will be in how you lovingly, strategically discipline them.

Ununified Parenting is when you don't agree in your parenting strategies. When you allow your children to see this, they will play each parent against the other. If you have been a parent very long, you have most likely witnessed this already. It is a must that you stand unified in front of your children when it comes to your disciplinary actions. I believe one of the greatest challenges is for divorced parents. Your children, especially as they get older, will learn to play one parent against the other. They will try their very best to divide and conquer. "Dad said he would buy that for me," or "Mom said I could go. You're so mean!" If your marriage did not stay together and you do not like your ex-spouse, for the sake of your kids, do everything you can to parent together. Teach your children to respect the other parent whether you do or not. This is good for them in most cases because it could undermine their own self-worth or identity as that parent's child.

Blended families are another challenge for having unified parenting. If you have married someone and you both have children, please never use the term your kids or my kids. When you decided to get married to each other, all the kids are your kids together. When you said, "I Do", you become one flesh; no longer is there yours and mine, they are ours. As a married couple bringing two families together, sit down, pray, and agree on your parenting TOGETHER!

Our youngest daughter Chloe had a cat when she was little. She wanted to bring the cat inside our home. Her mom told her that she could have it inside for a few minutes, but after that, she would have to put her cat outside on the porch. To say the least, Chloe was not happy. She proceeded to tell her mom, "What if Daddy tells me to bring it in, and I have to disobey you?" Shanda told her that your daddy would not do that because I told him where I stood on the matter, and we work together as a team.

It is our responsibility as parents to do our very best to keep a unified front for our kids, and if you need to disagree (which you will at some point), do it behind closed doors. Always stand unified in front of your kids. My prayers are with you if you are a single parent because you are making all the decisions without the other parent present to have your back. It can surely be exhausting. And being a stepparent has its challenges as well, but you keep the unified front in front of the children. You will have to let them know when your stepchildren are at your home, "This is how things will go while you are here." Lay out agreed upon clear plans and boundaries for house and relationship rules, and stick with it.

The Goal of Godly Discipline

The ultimate purpose of discipline is not behavior modification but heart transformation. It's about helping children develop a sense of accountability and to learn to make wise, God-honoring choices. Your children need to understand the consequences of sin and the beauty of grace. Discipline rooted in God's Word goes beyond external actions to address the heart, fostering a desire to honor God in all things. God expects our obedience, and we should expect obedience from our kids. We should also expect cheerful obedience from our children.

As parents, we are to discipline more for attitude than for actions. You may wonder what I mean. Yes, you want their actions changed, but their attitude is so important as well. In parenting, you may get outward obedience, but your children will still have inward rebellion. So, many times after we would correct our daughters for some kind of misbehavior, their demeanor would not be good at all.

Many times, we would make them retrace their steps if we got even a hint of attitude after they were corrected. We disciplined as much for attitude as we did for their actions because when their attitude is right, their actions would generally follow. We expected cheerful obedience from them.

Key Principles of Godly Discipline

Giving discipline God's way is with Love, not anger. I have been in ministry for a long time, and I have heard too many terrible regretful stories where parents would lose their cool with their children. Correct your children calmly and lovingly, never in anger. This reflects God's approach to us, firm but compassionate. Instead of yelling when your child disobeys, take a moment to pray for wisdom and respond with clarity and grace. I was taught a long time ago the difference between reacting and responding. When you react to your children's bad behavior, you might very well do something that you will regret. However, to respond is when you step back from the situation and proceed with Godly discipline in a loving way, not in anger.

It is too easy for us in everyday life situations to allow the disobedience of our children to get us really upset. Our goal is to focus on the heart, not just the behavior. Take the time to ask your child why they acted the way they did and address the underlying issue. This shifts the focus from punishment to growth. The outcome for your children is to help shape and mold them to become who God wants them to be. If your child lies, discuss why honesty is important to God and how lying can damage trust. All discipline is our opportunity as parents to teach them to do better and not be bad.

Every act of discipline is a chance to instill biblical values. Essentially, children are born with hell in them, a sin nature. It is your job to correct and train them, so the Holy Spirit is the dominant influence in their life instead of their flesh. After addressing disobedience, share a relevant Scripture like...

Ephesians 6:1 (NLT) "Children, obey your parents because you belong to the Lord, for this is the right thing to do."

Practical Approaches to Godly Discipline

Setting clear expectations with your children will keep them from saying, "I didn't know you wanted me to do the dishes." Instead, we can share clearer guidelines such as, "We don't interrupt when someone is speaking because it shows respect. If you interrupt, I will ask you to wait your turn before continuing." Clearly communicate rules and the consequences of breaking them so your children understand what is expected. Implementing common sense and logical consequences allows your children to experience the natural outcomes of their actions when appropriate. For intentional disobedience, apply consequences that match the behavior. If your child refuses to clean up their toys, they might lose the privilege of playing with them for a time. Be sure that through this process, you incorporate grace with them.

Teach your children about forgiveness and grace alongside discipline. Use moments of correction to point them to God's love. After enforcing a consequence, pray with your child and remind them that, just as God forgives us, you forgive them, too. You encourage your children for repentance and restoration. You help your child take responsibility for their actions, apologize, and make amends when necessary. If your child hurts a sibling, guide them to apologize sincerely and find a way to restore the relationship.

When one of my daughters got into trouble, I would take them to their bedroom and discipline them. Then, I talked to them about what they did wrong providing instructions of what not to do next time, and we would pray. Then, we would reconcile by telling them that I love and forgive them, giving them a hug and a kiss. My father used to say to me when I would get a whipping that it hurt him worse than it hurt me, and I thought to myself, no way!... until I became a father. It is so true, because I remember leaving their room with my heart hurting so badly.

However, I knew correction was best for them.
I think the pain goes both ways when we discipline our kids, but the pain of having prodigal children because we chose not to properly start early disciplining our children would be much worse. Discipline is correction motivated by our love. It is not something we do to them, it is something we do *for* them because we want to love them toward righteousness, knowing and serving Jesus Christ.

Discipline comes in variety of forms depending on your children's personalities. What works to correct bad behavior for one, may not work for another. Removal of privileges, a stern conversation, being sent to their room, or giving them a time out can work for different children. However, in our modern society, the choice of whippings is being equated to abuse or being done to children by the uneducated. Again, when it comes to discipline, we gave whippings in our home for our daughter's worse offenses. Yes, I know that this type of physical punishment is not a very popular or politically correct stance. But I am going to stand by the fact it's a biblically correct one, and it is one of the many effective ways to discipline. We tried our best not to use our hands when our girls disobeyed. Again, we will take them into the bedroom, we would decide their discipline, loss of privileges, added duties, or in the worst-case scenario, a whipping.

I remember vividly to this day a time when our youngest daughter, Chloe, got into trouble that warranted a whipping. She was about four years old and just her knowing that a whipping was coming was more terrifying in her little mind than the act of it. My wife Shanda knew I was getting soft in my discipline because it really did break my heart to do it. However, I knew it was best and would follow through. After I told Chloe she was getting a whipping and to come to me she kept stalling, asking to go potty and then going to her room first. Waiting for her to return to me was taking a while. Smiling at one another, Shanda and I knew she was up to something, but we agreed to wait a few more moments as she was telling me, "I'll be there in just a minute."

After some time, though, I began getting frustrated because she said this several times. Finally, she came to me and looked like a little Michelin Woman, you know the character for Michelin tires but as a little girl. Her butt was sticking out so far where she had put on about six pull ups over her butt. We could not help but laugh, and we tried not to. Her punishment that day was probably the least she had ever received because of her wittiness to shield against any pain.

India is pouting because she didn't get something her way!

Here is an article called ***"Children and the Rod of Correction"*** by Dave Miller Ph. D.…

"American civilization has undergone tremendous social shifting in the last fifty years in virtually every facet of its culture. This transformation is evident, for example, in the area of the family and parental discipline. From the beginning of this nation, most Americans have believed in the value of corporal punishment. This discipline has included spanking the child using a variety of instruments, including a "switch," paddle, razor strap, yardstick, belt, or hand. The last generation to have experienced this approach to parenting on a wide scale was the World War II generation. Due to the adverse influence of social liberals and alleged "specialists" in human behavior and child psychology, the thinking of many Americans has now been transformed to the extent that corporal punishment has come to be viewed as "child abuse" — even by the judiciary. Make no mistake: genuine child abuse is taking place every day in America. Some parents are burning, torturing, and even killing their children. However, the abuse of a good thing is no argument against its legitimate and judicious use. Extreme behavior often elicits an extreme reaction. We must not "throw out the baby with the bathwater." Regardless of the superficial appeal of the arguments that are marshaled against spanking, those who recognize that the Bible is the inspired Word of God are more concerned with biblical insight regarding the matter."

I hated disciplining my daughters, it really did hurt me more than them!

On another note, the Bible refers to physical discipline in Proverbs 13:24, 22:15, 23:13-14. When the Bible refers to the rod, in the Hebrew language, it is referring to tree branches for discipline. So, there are various ways of corrective measures to discipline children when they disobey. As a parent, be sure to pray and seek God with your children as to what will work to bring correction and what won't.

The Balance of Discipline and Relationship

Discipline should never overshadow the relationship you have with your child. Your connection with them must remain strong, even in moments of correction. You continually affirm your love for you children. Reassure your child that discipline doesn't change your love for them. Stay engaged with them by spending time building a relationship with your child outside of those disciplinary moments. Always be approachable as a parent to your children. Create an environment where your children feel safe coming to you, even when they've made mistakes. There will also be common challenges when it comes to discipline.

As a parent, disciplining your children is really exhausting. Shanda and I found this out firsthand. Keep in mind, that parenting is a marathon, not a sprint. Seek strength from God and support from your friends and church family when discipline feels overwhelming. Also seek the Lord in prayer: "Lord, give me wisdom and patience to guide my child as You guide me." If you have been a parent for any length of time, children will repeat the same mistakes. Remember that growth takes time. Continue to address the behavior while trusting God to work in their heart. Discipline will lead to conflict, so stay calm and remain focused on the goal of teaching, not winning an argument. Again, you are raising a future adult.

Reflection Questions:

1. Are there areas in your discipline where you need to be more consistent or loving?

2. How can you incorporate God's Word into moments of correction?

3. Are you addressing the heart behind your child's behavior, or just the actions?

A thought to remember…

Godly discipline is one of the greatest gifts you can give your child. It teaches them accountability, shapes their character, and points them to a loving God who desires their growth and flourishing. As you guide them with love, patience, and biblical truth, trust that God is using you to shape their hearts for His glory so they can become everything He created them for.

Chapter 5

Nurturing a Servant's Heart

Mark 10:45 (NLT) "For even the Son of Man came not to be served but to serve others and to give his life as a ransom for many."

"Only a life lived for others is a life worthwhile." Albert Einstein

To nurture a servant's heart in your children, it must begin in your own as a parent. When Shanda and I got married, our heart was for going to church and to serve the Lord. However, we immaturely thought serving the Lord was going to a church service. After all, that is what it was called, right? In our own personal ignorance, we thought we were being faithful servants of the Lord by going and sitting on a pew, singing praises to Jesus, and going home. When God called me to preach the gospel and I began to go to school to learn more about ministry, I had an eye-opening experience as to what serving the Lord, church, and the community was all about.

Understanding the importance of having a servant's heart would be life-changing to say the least for my family's future. God called us to start Freedom Church in the year 2000. Having a heart to serve would have been an understatement when it came to launching a brand-new church. It was to say the least an "All-hands-on-deck attitude" to see this new work for God not only launch but to actually succeed for the kingdom of God. It was a daunting task to cast vision and get other Christians on board to get this new church up and going. What Shanda and I didn't realize in the process was the impact that it was having on our three daughters. In a world that often prioritizes self-promotion and personal gain, teaching your children to have a servant's heart is a countercultural but essential aspect of raising Godly adults. A servant's heart reflects the humility and love of Christ, putting others' needs above one's own and seeking to glorify God in all actions.

As a family, after the first Sunday of starting Freedom Church on March 3rd, 2002, we had to rise really early (usually about 5:00am) on Sundays to go and set up our portable church in Hendersonville High School Auditorium. To our surprise, our daughters did not complain. They would help setup for us and have church with a spirit of anticipation of how God would move that day. Through this season, Shanda and I witnessed our daughters fall in love with the church and do their part to ensure we had our church ready to go each Sunday. God was instilling in them his spiritual DNA of serving. Nurturing this attitude in your children equips them to lead with love, compassion, and a sense of purpose. It also prepares them to live out their faith in tangible ways, making a meaningful impact on the world around them.

This impact of having a servant's heart was never more self-evident than in our youngest daughter Chloe, who was five years old. She wanted to start a ministry. She called it "Treasures of the Heart." Chloe had memory verses in this box that she would give to any of her church peers to take home to memorize. If they brought the verse back the next Sunday and could recite the verse by memory, then they would get a prize from the Treasure Box. Wow, we saw a spirit of excitement exuding from Chloe's spirit as she continued this newfound love for helping others memorize the heart of God, His Word. This was just the beginning of the servant's hearts we would see come to fruition in all three of our daughter's lives.

When we think of anyone serving in any capacity, what does a servant's heart look like? A child with a servant's heart demonstrates humility. As a parent, we lead our children through being an example of the utmost humility. The only characteristic that Jesus ever referred to himself in the Bible was in Matthew 11:29 when He said, "I am humble and gentle at heart." Humility is so important when it comes to a servant's heart. I have witnessed way too many times when Christians would start ministries or serve in any way, they would suffer getting puffed up with pride as if they were really something. This is not good at all for God's Kingdom. We should always remember that serving is about putting others first and recognizing that all gifts and opportunities come from God.

In ministry and in our daily lives as a Christian family, we would live out a spirit of empathy. We would be sure we were caring deeply about the needs and feelings of others. There were so many acts of ministering to others that our daughters were a part of which became a part of their hearts. So many acts of being generous to others was witnessed by our daughters. We wanted them to know that sharing their time, resources, and talents is what we do as God's servants without expecting anything in return. We want to be totally obedient to God in any way He wanted us to serve someone whether it was a neighbor, someone in our church, or in our community. Serving others is a form of worship, and serving others is a response to God's love in our own hearts.

Teaching children to serve others

Your example by modeling servanthood is the most powerful teacher you can have. Let your children see you serving others with joy and humility. You can help others out as a family. You may have a neighbor who is in need, and you could prepare a meal to take to them. Spend time praying as a family for those who are hurting. Involving your children in acts of service helps them become others centered which is a mark of spiritual maturity, not self-centeredness. Give your children hands-on opportunities to serve, both at home and in your community. I remember one Christmas season when our girls were growing up that Shanda was burdened about the homeless in the Nashville area. She wanted our girls to understand that Christmas was more than getting a bunch of gifts and that they needed to think of others. So, Shanda cut down on each of our daughters' Christmas budget to be able to purchase items for the Nashville homeless. We had always made financial donations to the Nashville Rescue Mission.

Shanda wanted us to go to Nashville as a family on Christmas morning to take care packets to the homeless people that we could find. Shanda did her research, purchased the different items, and we assembled the packets. We included socks, toothbrushes, toothpaste, wash clothes, brushes, combs, soap, lotion, lip balm, $5 gift cards and cash. We also gave them paper, a pen, and pre-postage paid envelops so they could reach out to anyone they knew. On Christmas morning, we went to Nashville with all our care packets to give out. We also took coats that we had as well as others that had been donated to us. So, even though I am the extravert in our family and Shanda is more the introvert, I watched my wife get out of the car and start handing out these packets with such love and boldness. Then, she sparked a fire in the rest of us, and we all followed suit. A spirit of joy suddenly rested on all of us when we saw the smiles of those we were giving these packets to. The homeless people were so appreciative of what we were giving them. To see their humble spirits being lifted on Christmas morning was such a wonderful sight to behold.

When we were getting to the point of handing out everything we had assembled and brought with us, we all had a sense of sadness that we didn't have more to give. Each of our daughters saw what serving others was all about. When it came down to giving out our last packet, one man came up to me and said, "I have a coat, but my friend doesn't have a coat. Do you have one?" We had just given out the last coat we had. However, I had on my UT Vols Starter coat. If you don't know, I am a diehard University of Tennessee Volunteers football fan, and that jacket was a Christmas gift to me the year before. But I couldn't stand the thought of someone not having a coat during the cold, so I quickly pulled it off and gave it to the guy. My girls were surprised that I did that since, "My blood runs orange." When I got back in the car and we proceeded to leave, I broke down and started crying realizing just how blessed we are as a family and what a blessing it was to go and serve others on Christmas morning.

Shanda's love for serving these homeless people made a tremendous impact on our entire family as we all took part in serving them. After that Christmas morning serving the homeless in Nashville, I cast the vision to our church. We went to serve them the next two Christmases with as many as over a hundred people showing up to go. Entire families were going to take part in giving out care packets, coats, food, and clothing. Serving the homeless, children in foster care, juveniles in the juvenile detention centers, and those that are incarcerated in our local county jail are a few ways we serve our community personally and through our church family.

Families of Freedom Church on Christmas morning praying before going to Nashville to serve the homeless.

Whenever you show your children the example of serving others, it will touch their hearts in a way that can continue on in their lives. Encourage them to help with household chores, being a part of serving at a church event, in the ministries of your church, or participate in a community outreach project. All our daughters grew up serving in our church family. They were on a journey to discover how they were uniquely gifted to share and serve by God.

Our oldest daughter Lily began to pursue singing to help with our church worship. She started in the youth worship team. Lily served in our church helping in the office for her senior year project. Leading worship is still her hearts passion and still serves in this area of her ability to this day. Lily now serves as a pastor's wife alongside of her husband, Cody.

India, our middle daughter, served in different capacities in our church growing up. As she became an adult, she wanted to start discipling other young girls in our church. Later, she came on staff for over five years leading our discipleship ministry. India shares the gospel in many different avenues. She now leads a ministry she started called "Daughters of Compassion" where this ministry helps teenagers who are aging out of foster care to find homes and job placement.

Chloe, our youngest daughter, began to serve our church in hospitality, the children's ministry, the youth worship team, and then helping in the creative and technical ministry of the church on staff for over 10 years. She now leads a small group study for home school moms through our church and our community.

Your children will take ownership of serving as they watch you serve. When you have your family devotions with them, you can highlight Biblical examples of serving. Teach your children about people in Scripture who served others selflessly, such as Jesus washing the disciples' feet (John 13:1-17) or the Good Samaritan (Luke 10:25-37). Encourage your children to always have a grateful heart because gratitude fosters generosity and a willingness to serve. Help your children recognize their blessings and see service as a way to share God's goodness with others. Also, during family devotions, list things you're grateful for and brainstorm ways to bless others with what God has given you.

Teaching Servanthood at Home

Promoting teamwork in serving at home with your family is essential. Teach your children that serving begins at home by helping one another with daily responsibilities. Shanda and I have built several homes especially while our daughters were growing up. After a few of our home sales, Shanda decided to get her own realtor license. Getting our home ready for a showing was a daunting task to say the least. Shanda had learned a phrase in her realtor training that our daughters and I knew quite well, "Realtor Ready." This meant it was all-hands-on-deck to get our home ready to be seen by potential buyers.

Teamwork had to make the dream work of selling this current home to build another one. Our daughters would work hard to do their part as much as their mother and me. As a family, working together to achieve a common goal builds unity and teaches work ethic. Encourage older siblings to help younger ones with homework or involve everyone in cleaning up after dinner. Be creative in ways to involve the entire family in helping one another.

Of course, there were times of our daughters complaining on another sibling about what they were doing or not doing. We tried our best to create a culture of kindness emphasizing the importance of speaking and acting with kindness toward each other in our family. Shanda and I would often witness "cat spats" between our daughters. We taught them to resolve conflicts with grace and to look for ways to encourage one another. If they couldn't resolve it, we stepped in. It is important to help your children learn to resolve their own conflicts because one day they will be on their own. Observe them in their resolution and help guide them when needed.

We would celebrate when we, as a family, got our home ready to be shown to buyers and shared in being grateful for each other's hard work. Always recognize and praise your children when they serve selflessly and most of all, serve others selflessly. "I noticed how you helped your brother clean up their toys without being asked. That's exactly what it means to have a servant's heart!" Encouragement goes along way. It might not seem like it in the moment but raising the praise for good deeds done can lifts the spirits of your children and anyone around you.

Cultivating a Global Perspective

With Shanda and me being in ministry for a long time, we have always been mission driven. After all, starting a brand-new church was all about reaching people who didn't have a relationship with Jesus. Local missions, foreign missions, and everywhere in between is the heart of the gospel. Cultivating a global perspective on serving was near and dear to our hearts, especially to teach our daughters to selflessly serve. As parents, we wanted them to know just how blessed they were to live in the United States. So, we had a mission trip planned at Freedom Church while our younger two daughters, India and Chloe, were still at home to go to the Dominican Republic. Our church financially supported a missionary there, so we took a team of people there to serve for a week. As parents, watching our daughter's experience was eye opening for them to say the least. This trip really helped solidify for our girls just how blessed they were.

There is a thought that when people go on a foreign mission trip that they will be a blessing to those they serve. However, what they discover is how much serving those that are marginalized has truly blessed themselves even more. Teach your children about mission work. This will introduce your children to have a grateful spirit about their blessings. If you can, when your children are old enough, go with them on a foreign mission trip with organizations that serve globally. Support a missionary as a family and involve your children in writing letters or praying for their ministry. Encourage a heart of generosity beyond the local community. Teach your children to think globally by supporting causes like clean water projects, sponsoring a child, or packing shoeboxes for children with Samaritan's Purse Operation Christmas Child.

India holding a baby from the Dominican Republic.

Chloe playing with the Dominican Republic kids blowing bubbles.

Pray for our world that is in need by making it a habit to pray as a family for specific needs around the world.

The Balance Between Serving and Rest

While teaching children to serve is important, it's equally vital to help them understand the need for rest and renewal. Even Jesus took time away to pray and recharge…

Mark 1:35 (NLT) *"Before daybreak the next morning, Jesus got up and went out to an isolated place to pray."*

Teach your children to serve joyfully but not out of obligation or exhaustion. Help them say no when it is necessary. You cannot serve joyfully if you are serving from an empty spiritual cup.

Teach your children to discern when to say no to protect their time with God, their family, and their personal growth. Also, as I shared in chapter one about "Building a Faith Foundation," I want to reemphasize that you teach your children the importance of the Sabbath. Yes, being at church each week is a command, and it is for your personal spiritual nourishment. A weekly Sabbath is for your own benefit. It is your opportunity to reflect on the past week and refocus on your priorities with God. Explain that rest is not selfish but part of God's design for a healthy, balanced life.

Reflection Questions:

1. How can you model a servant's heart for your children in daily life?

2. What opportunities for service can you create as a family?

3. How can you help your children balance serving others with caring for their own spiritual and emotional needs?

A thought to remember:

A servant's heart reflects Christ's love and humility. By teaching your children to serve with joy and compassion, you are equipping them to live out their faith and make a difference in the lives of others. There is a non-profit organization and multimedia movement started in 2008 called, "I am Second." It was started by Norm Miller, CEO of Interstate Battery System of America. This movement aims to inspire people to put Jesus Christ first in their lives. The movement is based on the idea of putting others and God first, and oneself second.

I am in no way dissing this concept because we are to always put Jesus Christ first. However, we cannot share the number one spot with him. Others would be second and let us ourselves be third! May we teach our children to always put God first, others second, and oneself next. If they learn this, they will discover the true fulfillment that comes from living a life of service.

Chapter 6

Raising Leaders who follow Jesus

1 Timothy 4:12: "Don't let anyone think less of you because you are young. Be an example to all believers in what you say, in the way you live, in your love, your faith, and your purity."

"Train up a child in the way he should go, but be sure you go that way yourself." Charles Spurgeon

Leadership is rooted in faith. Every child has the potential to lead, whether in their family, school, church, or future workplace. However, the kind of leadership that honors God is different from the world's definition. Leadership in God's kingdom is grounded in humility, service, and a desire to follow Christ's example.

After Shanda, me, and our team of adults started Freedom Church, we were leading everyone from a portable church to bricks and mortar. Through this process, we didn't realize how much of an impact our leadership had on our three daughters. Of course, as John Maxwell says, "Leadership is Influence," and that influence began in our home teaching them to take their personal responsibilities serious. They all three jumped in to not only help where they were needed in our new church plant, but they also would take the lead where they could. Leading our daughters by our serving example and giving them the vision of what we were trying to accomplish for the Lord made a difference in their hearts to serve.

Chloe was going on five years old at the launch of Freedom Church. She was about 10 years old in her old soul mindset. Chloe took the initiative to start helping watch children in the high school where we had church. You must understand, the kids she helped watch were twice her age, and they loved and respected Chloe. Of course, this was during the times of the set up and tear down process of our church with all the adult volunteers who had kids running around everywhere. Chloe's older two sisters, Lily and India, also took initiative to do what they could to ensure that anything that needed to be done, you could count on them.

Raising leaders who follow Christ isn't about teaching children to seek power or prestige but about helping them embrace their God-given gifts using them to influence others for His glory. True leadership begins with submission to God and a willingness to lead by example. Leadership is taught and caught.

Qualities of a Christ-Centered Leader

It is important to teach our children that any leading we do at all is to be done with a spirit of humility recognizing that leadership is about serving others, not elevating oneself. Living in a way that reflects Christ's character, even when no one is watching. We taught our girls that whatever we do or whatever position God leads us in, it is not about us, it is all about Him. As a family, our faith walk with Jesus is always "Our Utmost for His Highest" trusting God's guidance and relying on His strength in decision-making. When starting this church, we wanted our entire family to know that it was about understanding and caring for the needs of others. However, as we were leading for Jesus and His church, we taught our daughters to have courage to always stand firm in faith, even when it's unpopular or difficult.

Teaching Leadership Through Example

Children learn to lead by observing the behavior of those around them. Parents, as primary role models, play a vital role in demonstrating Christ-like leadership in their own lives. Show your children that leadership is about serving others, just as Jesus did. Here is a great verse about Jesus' leading...

Matthew 20:28 (NLT) "For even the Son of Man came not to be served but to serve others and to give his life as a ransom for many."

Jesus gave His sinless blood for our sinfulness to purchase our freedom from sin. What a powerful example of His heart for others. Jesus is unmatched in His leadership of humility and love. As parents, you may not be involved in leading a church, but you can certainly start serving in church, take the time to help a struggling neighbor, volunteer in a community project, and involve your children in the process.

Whenever we lead in any capacity, through our example and through our teaching our children, always make decisions with integrity. Demonstrate honesty, even in small matters, and explain to your children why integrity matters to God. For example, if you make a mistake, admit it and ask for forgiveness, showing your children the value of accountability. As we are to walk by faith, not by sight, share with your children how you rely on God for wisdom and guidance in your decisions. Be sure whenever you are facing a family decision, pray together and ask for God's direction.

Practical Ways to Develop Leadership Skills

Encourage responsibility by giving your children age-appropriate tasks that require them to take ownership and see them through. Assign them roles such as leading a family prayer at the dinner table or in a family devotion time. You can also ask your children to lead a devotion at some point that will help them teach and learn effective communication especially when speaking to others. This will help your children develop the confidence to express their thoughts, ideas, and have courage through this experience. Teach them to listen to others especially their siblings in a group setting with respect. Encouraging your children to think critically and find solutions to challenges they will inevitably face is crucial. When our daughters would come home and proceed to tell us about a problem they had encountered at school, we would guide them to brainstorm and evaluate possible solutions before stepping in to help.

There were times when Lily, India, or Chloe would share with Shanda and I a problem that they had experienced. We had to be sure not to allow the Papa Bear and Momma Bear to rise up too quickly and take control of the situation.

As parents, we had to learn that we cannot help our daughters lead through any problem or circumstance that they will face in the future if we jump in to rescue them. Yes, this is tempting to parents. We absolutely love them. However, there will come a day when they will be leading on their own, so let us equip them now for later. Trust me, I know how it feels to see them face those situations you would like to rectify. Middle school was the worst drama we faced with our daughters to help them through, but helping them learn to help themselves was the very best decision.

Highlighting some of the Godly leaders' lives in the Bible, such as Moses, Esther, Nehemiah, and most of all Jesus Himself, would be great for family devotions. You can discuss the qualities that made them effective leaders. One example that I have shared with my daughters is what I call the "Jethro Technique." In Exodus chapter 18, Moses' father-in-law saw how Moses was hearing all the Israelites complaints. They were lined up in front of Moses from morning till evening. And this is what Jethro saw and said…

Exodus 18:14 (NLT) "When Moses' father-in-law saw all that Moses was doing for the people, he asked, "What are you really accomplishing here? Why are you trying to do all this alone while everyone stands around you from morning till evening?"

So, Moses proceeds to tell Jethro how the people come to him to get their disputes settled, and he informs them of God's decision teaching them the laws and instructions. Then Jethro gives to Moses his rebuttal…

Exodus 18:17-19 (NLT) "This is not good!" Moses' father-in-law exclaimed. ¹⁸ "You're going to wear yourself out – and the people, too. This job is too heavy a burden for you to handle all by yourself. ¹⁹ Now listen to me, and let me give you a word of advice, and may God be with you. You should continue to be the people's representative before God, bringing their disputes to him."

Jethro went on to tell Moses to continue leading the people by sharing God's ways, giving them instructions on how to conduct their lives. However, he needed to select capable Godly people and appoint them to settle the smaller disputes. The major cases would be brought to Moses. These people would help him carry the load and make the task of leading everyone much easier. This is what Jethro said…

Exodus 18:23-24 (NLT) If you follow this advice, and if God commands you to do so, then you will be able to endure the pressures, and all these people will go home in peace." ²⁴ Moses listened to his father-in-law's advice and followed his suggestions.

Shanda and I have had the privilege to watch our daughters lead in different aspects. When they were small, we would give them things to do at home and work with their siblings. They would lead at church in our children's ministry or in projects at school when other students were involved. As our daughters grew, their leadership opportunities expanded. They helped lead in school clubs, at church in worship, with small groups, and began ministries by casting vision with others to be involved.

Lily leading worship for the student ministry at Freedom Church.

Look for ways your children can take on leadership roles in their church, school, or community. Encourage them to organize a charity drive, lead a prayer group, or mentor younger children in a hobby or skill. All of your children will grow up if you keep feeding them. They will need leadership skills in life to not only succeed but to also learn how to work with others to accomplish any endeavor.

Teaching Servant Leadership

One of the most crucial aspects of Godly leadership is servanthood. Teach your children to lead by putting others first and prioritizing their needs. Leadership is always by example! Make service a regular part of your family life to reinforce the idea that leadership is about helping others. Volunteer at a food bank or participate in a church mission trip as a family like I shared in the previous chapter.

Whenever we would see a need as a family, we taught our daughters to jump in and help out. Praise your children when they take initiative to help others, no matter how small the act may seem. Teach your children to show gratitude when they are able to get others involved for any kind of project or work, especially if teamwork is involved.

Teaching your children to acknowledge the contributions of others and to work collaboratively is such a beautiful sight to behold when they are accomplishing a common goal.

India sharing a Word for the Lord at Freedom Church.

Challenges of Leadership

Leadership often comes with challenges, such as criticism, failure, or the temptation to compromise values. Help your children navigate these challenges by equipping them to have an understanding that the difference between a leader and a follower is that the leader does not quit. A leader is resilient despite any setbacks they will face. Help your children understand that failure is part of growth, and God uses setbacks to strengthen their character and set them up for future success. Share how you overcame a personal failure by trusting God and persevering.

Chloe leading worship for the student ministry at Freedom Church.

One of the greatest challenges of leadership that we face as adults, and not to mention of children, is equipping them how to handle criticism. I know from personal experience that for Shanda and me leading a church for almost a quarter of a century, if you are not getting criticized, it is because you are not doing anything. Teach your children to respond to criticism with humility, grace, and discernment.

Encourage them to pray about feedback they receive and seek wisdom on how to respond. You will have to remind your children that when they are criticized, those moments may cause pain, but it is not a reflection of who they are in Jesus Christ. Yes, you always want to see if there is any merit to the criticism or look at what you can learn to do better. However, remind them that their identity is in Christ alone. It is paramount that as parents, you ground your children's confidence in their identity as God's children, not in their accomplishments or titles.

Reflection Questions:

1. How can you model servant leadership for your children?

2. What leadership opportunities can you provide for your children in your home, church, or community?

3. How can you help your children develop the courage to stand firm in their faith as leaders?

A thought to remember...

Shanda and I prayed for our daughters from the time they came in the world to be world changers for Jesus, but mostly, to be found in His will for them to live out their purposes. Does this mean that as they lead in their perspective places God has them that their names will be recognized by the masses? Not at all. Whether they were wives, homemakers, parents, ministry leaders, or professionals in the marketplace, we wanted to help prepare them to lead where God leads them to be only in the center of His will.

Raising leaders who follow Christ goes beyond merely equipping them with practical leadership techniques; it is about nurturing their hearts to reflect Christ-like character. True leadership rooted in faith requires instilling values of service, humility, and love, guiding them to prioritize God's will over personal ambition.

By fostering a deep, personal relationship with God, you help them build a foundation that enables their leadership to be transformative, not only in their own lives but also in the lives of those they lead. This kind of leadership has an eternal perspective, focusing on advancing God's kingdom by pointing others to Him through their actions, decisions, and influence. In this way, leadership becomes a form of ministry, where their impact is measured not just by worldly success but by their ability to inspire others to walk closer with Christ.

Chapter 7

Teaching Resilience in Faith

Romans 5:3-4 (NLT) "We can rejoice, too, when we run into problems and trials, for we know that they help us develop endurance. 4 And endurance develops strength of character, and character strengthens our confident hope of salvation."

"God never said that the journey would be easy, but He did say that the arrival would be worthwhile." Max Lucado

One thing that stands true about life is that it is daily! No matter if you are a Christ follower or not, everyone faces adversity in life. Understanding resilience from a Biblical perspective is the ability to bounce back from difficulties, setbacks, and challenges.

In today's world, where children face numerous pressures, resilience is a vital quality for navigating life's uncertainties. As Christian parents, teaching resilience means guiding our children to develop a deep-rooted faith that sustains them through trials.

Resilience is not just about overcoming adversity; it's about trusting God's promises, finding strength in His presence, and developing a lasting hope. When we teach our children to rely on God's strength, they learn to endure difficulties with grace and faith, rather than be overwhelmed by them.

Why Resilience Matters

Shanda and I had a front row seat while raising our daughters seeing what they faced, and we knew we had to help them face challenges with confidence. If you are a parent and have been a parent very long, you know what I am talking about. Resilience prepares our children to handle disappointments, failures, and hardships without losing their sense of purpose.

Our oldest daughter Lily was a cheerleader two years in middle school. When she entered high school, she tried out for the cheerleading squad. She prepared with hope for the day of the try outs. When the list was posted of who made the squad, Lily's name was not on there. She came home with such a spirit of feeling rejected. Lily felt insecure during the try outs because she felt her back-handspring was not great. We were not sure if Lily's gymnastic abilities were strong enough, but either way, she did not make the team.

When Shanda and I learned that she did not make it, we encouraged Lily attempting to guide her as we empathized with her in this reality. First, we shared with her and with our other daughters in any tough circumstance that this must not be God's will. Second, we wanted our girls in any situation to seek the Lord, "What is God trying to teach you?" Third, we wanted them to know that when something does not work out the way they wanted it to, God must have something better in store for them. Last, we would encourage them to pray for understanding for what God had for them. His plan for us is always perfect. I love the following verse from Jeremiah.

Jeremiah 29:11 (NLT) "For I know the plans I have for you," says the LORD. "They are plans for good and not for disaster, to give you a future and a hope."

When a child faces rejection or a tough school situation, our job as parents is to be their number one cheerleader to encourage them that they can turn to God's promises for comfort and guidance. God's plans for us are always good for a future and a hope. The enemy will always try to get anyone, especially our kids as they are growing up in life and in faith, to blame God instead of turning to God in hard circumstances that will take place.

Each situation that our children face in their formable years is where we as parents help them build spiritual and emotional maturity. A resilient faith equips children to trust God in difficult times and to see challenges as opportunities for growth.

At times, Shanda and I would sense our daughter's heart break in different circumstances when they faced rejection. They would oftentimes compare themselves to others which we understood because we've all had those thoughts at some point when others got something we wanted or were pursuing. This instance is a great time to share with your child how God used a personal challenge to strengthen your faith and draw you closer to Him. God is far too creative to make us all the same so we can learn to have a heart that celebrates the uniqueness of others realizing that we are uniquely created, too.

We as parents, tried our best to help prepare our daughters for life's ups and downs. I have always said, "You are coming out of a problem, in a problem, or a problem is coming." Teaching resilience helps children develop the mental and emotional flexibility to adapt and thrive in changing circumstances. Help them see how God works through trials to refine and develop their character, as stated in the book of James in the Bible...

James 1:2-4 (NLT) Dear brothers and sisters, when troubles of any kind come your way, consider it an opportunity for great joy. ³ For you know that when your faith is tested, your endurance has a chance to grow. ⁴ So let it grow, for when your endurance is fully developed, you will be perfect and complete, needing nothing.

Kids are going to face rejection as they grow up. It is a part of life! Whether it is not being picked for the team, losing a friendship, or struggling with school challenges. James reframes trials as opportunities for growth rather than purely negative experiences. For kids, this means understanding that rejection can teach them resilience, help them discover their unique strengths and shapes in their identity.

Developing Resilience Through Faith

Shanda and I knew as we raised our three daughters that there were three sets of eyes always watching us. We faced our share of setbacks and disappointments; however, we tried very hard to always model to our girls that our full trust was in God no matter what. Your example of faith during difficult times is one of the most powerful ways to teach resilience.

I remember a very difficult time for us as a family. Freedom Church was meeting in the Hendersonville High School Auditorium for our Sunday church service each week. We had been there for over four years. The Sumner County Board of Education told me in a board meeting that Freedom Church had to stop meeting there. We only had a few months to find a new home.

As a family, we prayed for God to give us His direction of what to do. We knew God wanted His church to continue. I tried to find places to lease for us to meet as a church, but to no avail. We had closed on our property that we had purchased. So, Shanda and I knew our girls could see the spiritual battle we were facing and the pressure to move forward as a church. God began to open doors, move on people's hearts, and He worked through our church family as I led a building project on our land.

The Freedom Church family moved into our new church home within three days of our eviction from the high school. This was a personal story of God's faithfulness through challenging times, demonstrating trust in His plans for our daughters to witness. This is just one example of them watching God's faithfulness that would build up their faith for their future challenges.

Show your kids through your life's examples as they grow up by encouraging them in Gods ways to have a growth mindset. Help your children see failures as opportunities to learn and grow rather than reasons for despair. When they struggle with schoolwork, praise their effort and encourage them to keep trying, knowing God is with them. When they are discouraged, teach them to turn to Scripture to equip your children with Bible verses that remind them of God's love, promises, and strength.

One verse that we taught our daughters to memorize that would encourage them to not be overcome with circumstances and situations that will always come their ways is...

Philippians 4:13 (NLT) "For I can do everything through Christ who gives me strength."

I remember sharing with our daughters and our congregation at Freedom Church to say this powerful verse in segments, "For I can – Do everything – Through Christ – Who gives me strength!" As it has been said, "can't; never did anything". So, encourage your children not to ever allow anything that takes place to make them feel like a victim but to live in victory through the strength of Jesus Christ!

Teaching our children to have a strong intimate prayer life is crucial. We wanted, as parents, to build into our daughters' lives the power through prayer. We knew they would one day launch from our home and would need to know they can access the very Creator who spoke their lives into existence and help them in their journey of life. So, encourage your children to pray regularly about their fears, struggles, and concerns. Make prayer a part of daily routines, whether before a challenging school day or after a frustrating experience.

It is paramount who our children have as their peers. They need a network of fellow friends that are a part of a community of faith where your children feel supported and encouraged. That is why regularly attending church, church activities, and youth groups is so vital to the resilience of the faith of our children. Here is another verse we taught our daughters that is important for faith vitality…

Hebrews 10:25 (NLT) "And let us not neglect our meeting together, as some people do, but encourage one another, especially now that the day of his return is drawing near."

As parents, our example and leadership in attending church is important. May it never be optional but consistent. A church family can be an environment with other believers where not only us, but also our children, can have positive influence. A church family is a place where our children can learn who God is, His love for them, and His expectations for their lives. Remember, when you take your family to church, your children see you as parents who are worshipping, praying, and serving together. This models for your children the importance of prioritizing God in their own lives and demonstrates what it looks like to live a life of faith. So never be lackadaisical about offering a sense of belonging and spiritual growth with a church family that will build spiritual tenacity into your children's hearts and lives.

Practical Ways to Build Resilience

Teach your children that problems are an opportunity to be solved. Help your children learn to identify problems, evaluate their options, and take positive action. When they face a problem, work together to brainstorm solutions and consider the consequences of each choice. Most of all, reiterate about prayer, encourage them to ask God to give them clarity on future decisions.

I'll be the first to admit that raising girls and boys is different. However, both genders will deal with emotions. How we help them get through those times will be different for each child. Teaching your child to deal with their emotions when a situation arises can be really stressful as a parent. Equip your children with strategies to manage their emotions during those often-stressful situations. First of all, Shanda and I would give our daughters reassurance that it is okay to not be okay, but it is not okay to stay that way. We try to help them see the situation from a 30,000-foot view that no matter what has happened, it is not the end of the world. That it's only for a season, and it won't always be that way. First, we pray as a family when tensions rise that God is always there to help in any situation that happens.

Hebrews 4:16 (NLT) "So let us come boldly to the throne of our gracious God. There we will receive his mercy, and we will find grace to help us when we need it most."

It can be really tempting to try and work out the situations and circumstances that happen with our children. If you do that, you will miss the opportunity for your children to grow in their independence. Allow your children to face things that happen where you can help coach them through the challenges that build their confidence and problem-solving skills.

There are going to be those times, as parents, when you can teach through how you model resilience in conflict you will personally have. That will be important in demonstrating to your children about how to handle disagreements and conflicts with grace and forgiveness. Again, your children are watching you as parents on how you model forgiveness and healthy communication, and they are learning during disagreements with your spouse or other family members. One of the greatest boosts to your children's morale and attitude is to not miss celebrating victories no matter how small. Be sure to not only acknowledge but celebrate your child's efforts and achievements. Maybe you have one child who has struggled in a particular subject in school, and next thing you know, they bring home a letter grade higher than the last time. Always celebrate the wins as a family, together! Teach that we celebrate one another's wins. When your child is successful with a school presentation, the courage they showed in a difficult situation, or apologized for something they did wrong without having to be told, don't miss the win!

Overcoming Setbacks with Faith

Watching our children get hurt in life physically is a type of pain that heals up, and if there is a scar, it will be a constant reminder of what happened and to learn from it. When our children go through any kind of pain whether it is physical or emotional, we must teach them to process pain and disappointment. If Shanda and I had a dollar for each incident we watched our girls get hurt and cry, we would have a lot of money to say the least. Whether they were hurt physically or their heart was hurting from someone, we helped them understand and express their emotions healthily. Maybe something they desired and had prayed for did not happen. We would offer some guidance in understanding that when God answers "no," it must mean it wasn't His will for us. And for that, we can be thankful as we anticipate something better than our own plan must be coming ahead.

As parents, we would encourage our daughters to share their feelings in prayer and to write down how they feel. To help them build their faith when life would happen, we did not let them ever blame God for what they went through. Yes, God has big shoulders, and He can always handle our complaints. However, blaming God for how things work out is a faith growth mistake. In all facets of life, help your kids to see setbacks as a setup for a comeback.

Drive home in the hearts of your children that failures are a part of God's plan for their growth. One of many Biblical stories that you can share with your kids of setbacks is Joseph's betrayal in Genesis 37 and his journey to becoming a leader despite his trials. If anyone could be in a position to blame God, in my pastoral opinion, it was Joseph. You may not be completely familiar with his story, but many say he is Joseph with the coat of many colors. What is interesting is one verse in Psalm 105…

Psalm 105:19 (NLT) "Until the time came to fulfill his dreams, the Lord tested Joseph's character."

Even though Joseph was thrown in a pit, sold into slavery, falsely accused of rape, and yet later he became second in power under Pharaoh in Egypt, it was the Lord who allowed this. God will test us as parents, He will test our kids as they grow up. This gives us an opportunity to grow in resilience in our faith walk with Jesus. Remember, without being tested, there will be no testimony for Jesus!

Maybe you have heard the saying, "When life gives you lemons, make lemonade." Encourage your children to have this perspective of hope making the best out of any obstacle. You can, with God's help and direction, find a way to turn obstacles into something positive or beneficial. Be sure that no matter what your kids will go through, you emphasize that God uses all things for good (Romans 8:28) and that there is hope in every situation. Remind them of the resurrection story, where Jesus turned the ultimate defeat into the ultimate victory. Be a constant encourager to your children. Remind them that if they think they are beaten in life, then they kind of are, and that is not the response for anything they go through. No matter what the circumstances are, we have the opportunity to coach and lead our kids through it. God will always be faithful, so we are to be faithful to Him.

Check out the following verses of encouragement of God's faithfulness...

Psalm 34:17-18 (NLT) "The Lord hears his people when they call to him for help. He rescues them from all their troubles. 18 The Lord is close to the brokenhearted; he rescues those whose spirits are crushed."

Reflection Questions:

1. How do you model resilience in your own life for your children to see?

2. What specific scriptures can you share with your children to help them through difficult times?

3. How can you encourage your child to view challenges as opportunities for growth rather than obstacles?

A thought to remember...

Teaching resilience in faith is one of the greatest gifts you can give your child. It prepares them not only to face life's challenges but to emerge stronger, wiser, and more deeply rooted in Christ's love. By nurturing their faith and guiding them through trials with grace and courage, you're raising children who are spiritually resilient, ready to face the uncertainties of life with hope. Shanda and I always tell our kids to this day that God will always teach us something in the hard times that will strengthen us if we trust God no matter what!

Chapter 8

Encouraging a Heart of Gratitude

1 Thessalonians 5:18 (NLT) "Be thankful in all circumstances, for this is God's will for you who belong to Christ Jesus."

"It is only with gratitude that life becomes rich."
Dietrich Bonhoeffer

The power of gratitude is a foundational attitude in the Christian life, a crucial trait for raising spiritually healthy and emotionally resilient future adults. Cultivating a heart of gratitude in your children helps them to focus on God's blessings and trust His goodness, even in times of trial. A heart of gratitude fosters joy, humility, and contentment, while also helping guard against a spirit of entitlement and dissatisfaction.

Teaching gratitude involves more than simply reminding our children to say "thank you" or focusing on material blessings. It's about nurturing a deeper appreciation for God's provision, His love, and His work in their lives. When our children learn to give thanks in all circumstances, they develop a lasting sense of peace and fulfillment rooted in God's sovereignty.

Why Gratitude Matters

Reframing our children's perspective about where all their blessings flow from began with each of our daughters from the time they began to walk and talk. They were taught to honor and give constant gratitude to God who gives us His gift of blessings, and most of all, our breath and heartbeat of life....

James 1:17 (NLT) "Whatever is good and perfect is a gift coming down to us from God our Father, who created all the lights in the heavens."

Teaching gratitude helps children see life through a lens of abundance rather than scarcity. There is always a blessing to be grateful for in any given day if you look for it and teach your children to do the same. Help your child notice the good in everyday situations, like the beauty of a sunset or the kindness of a friend, instead of focusing solely on what they lack. An "It's Mine" mindset will be any child's focus as they relate to siblings, playmates, or when they begin pre-school.

Shanda and I saw first-hand how little humans want more and appreciate less. It was a constant teaching to help our daughters have a spirit of giving, not taking. Keeping their attitudes in check helped promote emotional well-being. A grateful heart enhances emotional health by reducing feelings of stress, anxiety, and comparison. It is not easy to be the parents who must constantly referee the "It's Mine" mindset; however, it will pay off in the long run.

We taught our daughters that the key to living a blessed life is having a heart of generosity. We are to be grateful for all of God's blessings and share them, too. Teaching kids to share is like pulling teeth it seems. So, as they grew, we taught our daughters that the first and the best always goes to God. We taught them the principle of tithing. If they received a dollar, a dime would go to the house of the Lord. We taught them that it did not matter how they received any kind of money whether it was a gift, birthday money, or doing any kind of chore around our house, we always show our gratitude to the Lord with the tithe because everything belongs to Him. So, tithing became a second nature to them as they grew and even to this day! I remember when they lived at home, they would be so excited to bring the tithe to the church with a heart of gratitude. We wanted our daughters to experience what Shanda and I have experienced our entire life. If you will give God the first and the best, He will bless the rest...

Proverbs 3:9-10 (NLT) "Honor the LORD with your wealth and with the best part of everything you produce.[10] Then he will fill your barns with grain, and your vats will overflow with good wine."

Even with our very best teaching for our children to have a heart of gratitude, the selfishness can creep back in through their humanness. I remember when Chloe was a little girl, and we were still taking her to trick or treat. I would take her to our family and friends. We would also go to the subdivisions where we knew that they would give out the good candy. I have always loved M&M's, Butter Finger candy bars, and Reese's Cups! On a particular evening after we went everywhere, Chloe had a brimming big bag of candy. You name it, it was in there. So, I asked Chloe to give me some M&M's, and she said, "No dad, It's mine." Excuse me? "No Dad, you will eat all of my chocolate." I told her I did not ask for all her candy, but I knew she had gotten some M&M's. Chloe could at least give me some M&M's for the taxi service.

What Chloe did not understand was this, I was the one who got her to the places to receive the M&M's. I was thinking, you ought to return to me the tithe of the M&M's. I am the one who made this possible. Also, if I had wanted to, I could forcibly take the M&Ms from her, and she would never get another pack of M&M's. She didn't understand that if I wanted to, I could go to the store and buy so many M&M's that she wouldn't be able to eat them and get a bellyache trying. Here is a principle we can learn, technically speaking, to not return the tithe to the Lord is stealing. It's taking what belongs to God!

I am glad to share that it didn't take long before Chloe learned that she really enjoyed sharing with others and giving. As a very young girl, she counted down the days until Sunday and every opportunity to be able to tithe. Giving offerings and gifts to those around her became a great joy in her life!

Shanda and I never wanted our daughters to rob God, but to bless Him back for all His blessings…

Malachi 3:8-10 (NKJV) "Will a man rob God? Yet you have robbed Me! But you say, 'In what way have we robbed You?' In tithes and offerings.[9] You are cursed with a curse, For you have robbed Me, Even this whole nation.[10] Bring all the tithes into the storehouse, That there may be food in My house, And try Me now in this," Says the LORD of hosts, "If I will not open for you the windows of heaven And pour out for you such blessing That there will not be room enough to receive it."

Shanda and I taught our daughters that you cannot outgive God. We have shown them this practice by our own example. God will open the windows of heaven and richly bless us all for bringing the tithe to His storehouse which is the local church. Watching our daughters from when they were small get excited to bring God's tithe to the church was so heartwarming to us. We taught them a threefold aspect of tithing to the Lord. First, tithing provides for God's work through His church. Second, tithing teaches us to always put God first. And third, tithing increases our faith in God. Showing our gratitude to God through tithing is a discipline that our daughters are obedient in showing God their heart of gratitude for all His bountiful blessings to this day. Teaching our children to be grateful for each day during family meals or bedtime prayers is a great way to encourage an attitude of appreciation as a lifestyle.

Showing gratitude to God in all aspects of life is a spiritual growth journey. Gratitude deepens our relationship with God, reminding us of His constant presence and faithfulness. Teaching your child to express gratitude to God in prayer for specific blessings and experiences reinforces the understanding that all good things come from Him (James 1:17).

Practical Ways to Teach Gratitude

I cannot reiterate how important it is that you model gratitude in your own life. The "Do as I say, not as I do" parenting philosophy does not work. Children learn gratitude by observing their parents' attitudes and actions. Show them how to express thanks in all circumstances. Express gratitude for the little things in life—whether it's a sunny day, a warm meal, or a good night's sleep. Share why these are blessings from God.

Create a daily practice of thankfulness. Establish routines that foster a heart of gratitude, such as sharing what each family member is grateful for at the dinner table or in daily prayers. Teach them to appreciate others as well. Encourage your children to thank others for their kindness and service. Help your kids learn to write thank-you notes or make cards for people who have blessed them, like their family, teachers at school, friends, their church teachers, and youth leaders. Also, gratitude is showing respect for those who are their elders. We tried to teach our daughters to always say, "Yes Sir, No Sir, Yes Ma'am, No Ma'am." They did not always get this right, sometimes it would seem their heart could have been saying it, yet it was never verbally conveyed. But they knew to show their thankfulness and respect to those in their lives who were good to them.

Help your children understand the difference between wants and needs. Teach them to find joy in what they have. Shanda and I know from experience that this is a challenge due to our desire to give our daughters everything they wanted if we could afford it. However, as Shanda has always said, "Too much of a good thing is not a good thing." In other words, sure, as parents, we want to bless our children but spoiling them with too much will backfire in the long run. So, we were consistently teaching our girls balance between "needs vs. wants" at home, discussing what is truly essential and what is extra.

What was most important in teaching and encouraging our daughters to have a heart of gratitude was help them find God's Hand in their daily lives. Make it a daily routine as your children grow to recognize and express gratitude for

God's provision and presence in the everyday. Help your children to see each and every day at least one thing they are thankful to God which shows them God's faithfulness.

Nurturing a Heart of Generosity

Connecting gratitude to giving in all aspects of our children's lives helps them understand that grateful hearts are also generous hearts. As I shared earlier about how Shanda and I taught our daughters to show God our utmost gratitude to Him through tithing to our church, you can also involve them in family charitable activities, like packing shoeboxes for Samaritans Purse Operation Christmas Child. Explain how these acts reflect God's love and provision. Teach them to give freely by encouraging your children to share their time, talents, and possessions with others. Help them donate old toys, clothes, or spend time volunteering at church, local shelters, or retirement homes.

Fostering a spirit of service in the hearts of our children will connect acts of service with a heart of gratitude. Show how serving others is a natural outflow of being thankful for God's grace. Shanda and I always incorporated serving as a form of our giving into the family's routine, such as preparing meals for a family in need or doing chores.

Overcoming Ungratefulness and Complaints

If we ever had one of our daughters in a stinky mood, we would tell them to tell God three things they were grateful for so they could turn those frowns into smiles. Also, we would teach them to pray when they were complaining or discontent. That was a great way to help change their attitude and perspective. Help your children recognize when they're feeling ungrateful and guide them to respond by turning to God in prayer. Encourage them to pray about their feelings of discontentment, and thank God for what they do have, fostering a habit of finding God's blessings in all circumstances. Life can throw us curve balls, and as adults, we can find ourselves doing the same things, such as complaining, all while we try to coach our children not to do that. Try your best to model to your children how to handle disappointments without grumbling, trusting God's wisdom and timing. Yes, if we are all honest, we have failed at this. However, when anything takes place to complain or grumble about, as parents may we ask, "What is God wanting to teach us?" This is a time where you can share stories of God's faithfulness through your own trials, helping them see how even unmet expectations is a part of life which can lead to growth and a new outlook.

Turning our complaints into praise to the Lord is a great mark of spiritual maturity. You may ask why? Someone in this world will always have it worse than our current circumstances and that is why it is crucial to help your children turn their complaints into expressions of gratitude. So, when they are complaining, grumbling, and expressing dissatisfaction, encourage them to think of something they're thankful for, prompting them to shift their focus from lack to the abundance of blessings they have!

Reflection Questions:

1. How can you model a heart of gratitude for your children?

2. What daily practices can you establish to nurture gratitude in your family?

3. How can you teach your children to cultivate an attitude of contentment?

A thought to remember...

Teaching gratitude is about more than just good manners; it is about instilling a deep-seated attitude of thankfulness that flows from a heart that is aligned with God's will. As parents, even in the tough times of life, we can find something to be grateful for. Teaching our children to do the same will be so beneficial for how they will navigate their future. As you nurture a heart of gratitude in your children, you're helping them develop a lasting sense of joy, peace, and contentment, anchored in the knowledge of God's love and provision. May your family grow in gratitude, honoring God in all circumstances and reflecting His goodness to the world.

Chapter 9

Biblical Identity & Future Adults

Galatians 3:26 (NLT) *"For you are all children of God through faith in Christ Jesus."*

"The Christian's identity is not found in what they do for Christ, but in what Christ has done for them." Dietrich Bonhoeffer

Understanding our identity in Christ is never more important than in the world we live in today. There is so much confusion and attacks on our children being brought about from Satan's ploy to kill, steal, and destroy (John 10:10). Empowering our children with a strong biblical identity is foundational for their spiritual health and well-being. A child's identity shapes their beliefs, values, and actions. When children understand their identity as children of God, they are more secure, resilient, and able to navigate the challenges of life. A biblical identity helps them see themselves as God sees them, loved, valued, and purposeful, regardless of their circumstances.

Teaching our children their identity in Christ is about affirming their worth, dignity, and purpose. It involves helping them understand that their identity is not based on what they do, how they look, or what others think of them. Instead, it is rooted in their relationship with Jesus Christ, who calls them His own. It is paramount to encourage and emphasize to our children everyday who they are and whose they are, and His name is Jesus!

Key Aspects of a Biblical Identity

As children of God, our identity is found in being God's beloved children! Using scripture to reinforce this truth not only in our children's lives, but also in our own lives, is to be a constant reminder such as…

John 1:12 (NLT) *"But to all who believed Him and accepted Him, He gave the right to become children of God."*

Help your child understand that their identity is secure in Christ alone. Their identity is not in what they think of themselves or what others may say. Shanda and I had a front row seat watching our daughters deal with what others would say to them or about them, especially in middle school. We would encourage them to not let what anyone says lodge into their hearts. If it didn't align with what they knew to be true and who God says they are, like being loved, chosen, and a masterpiece, then they would need to reject the hurtful and harmful intentions of others. Every time our children, or even we as adults, give weight to the words of others, we will miss what God's Word says about us. Every time we put our eyes on others, we take our eyes off God! We taught our girls to pray for those who may say or do things that are hurtful. Also, we all know in life, others may be dealing with their own pain, insecurities, and self-doubt. We are to love everyone and keep our hearts and minds on Christ.

Teaching our children about God's grace and forgiveness can never be emphasized enough. Throughout my ministry, I have witnessed the broken hearts of parents who have watched their kids search for their identity in the world. They make wrong decisions, hang with the wrong crowd, and seek the approval of those who are far from God. I have devoted chapter 11 on parenting prodigal kids if you have a wayward child or know of someone who does. Despite what mistakes that any kid will make in looking for their identity in the wrong places, continue loving them. Share with them that God loves them and how God is a God of redemption.

There is no greater illustration in the Bible of God's boundless love and forgiveness for us all than the prodigal son. The Parable of the Prodigal Son, found in Luke 15:11-32, is one of Jesus' most well-known teachings about God's grace, repentance, and restoration. The story follows a father with two sons. The younger son, eager for independence, demands his inheritance early leaving home to pursue a reckless, self-indulgent life. He squanders his wealth in wild living and soon finds himself destitute, working in a pigsty longing to eat the food given to the pigs.

In his desperation, he realizes his mistakes and decides to return home, hoping to be received as a servant rather than a son. However, his father, filled with compassion, runs to meet him, embraces him, and joyfully restores him to the family. He throws a great feast to celebrate his son's return, declaring, "for this son of mine was dead and is alive again; he was lost and is found." (Luke 15:24)

Meanwhile, the older brother, who has remained dutiful and obedient, becomes resentful of the celebration. He feels overlooked and complains that he has never been honored in the same way. The father gently reminds him that everything he has is already his, but it was necessary to celebrate because the lost son has returned. This is such a beautiful story of grace and forgiveness. The father represents God's unconditional love, always ready to forgive those who repent. This parable teaches that no matter how far we stray, God's love and mercy remain open to all who turn back to Him. I will discuss this further in chapter 11 from the perspective of those who are parenting prodigal kids.

We as parents need to try our very best to help our children know that no matter what, they are chosen and accepted by God and by us. That does not mean that we accept any bad behavior, but we help them grasp the concept of God's sovereign choice and their acceptance in Him.

Ephesians 1:4-5 (NLT) "Even before he made the world, God loved us and chose us in Christ to be holy and without fault in his eyes. ⁵ God decided in advance to adopt us into his own family by bringing us to himself through Jesus Christ. This is what he wanted to do, and it gave him great pleasure."

This scripture reinforces that they are chosen and accepted in God's family. Teach your child that they are loved by God's unconditional love. Teach them about the depth of God's love, such as these following verses...

Romans 8:38-39 (NLT) "And I am convinced that nothing can ever separate us from God's love. Neither death nor life, neither angels nor demons,[b] neither our fears for today nor our worries about tomorrow — not even the powers of hell can separate us from God's love. ³⁹ No power in the sky above or in the earth below — indeed, nothing in all creation will ever be able to separate us from the love of God that is revealed in Christ Jesus our Lord."
Not only is God's love for all of us inexhaustible, as we are living in Christ, help your children understand their identity is empowered by the Holy Spirit. After Christ's

resurrection, He was on the earth forty more days. Before Jesus ascended out of sight, He said these words...

Acts 1:8 (NLT) "But you will receive power when the Holy Spirit comes upon you. And you will be my witnesses, telling people about me everywhere — in Jerusalem, throughout Judea, in Samaria, and to the ends of the earth."

Practical Ways to Empower Their Identity in Christ

Teaching our children scripture to memorize into their daily life will reinforce their identity in Christ through God's promises. God's will comes through God's Word when we make it a priority. You can create a family memory verse for the month that emphasizes their identity in God, such as...

Psalm 139:14 (NLT) "Thank you for making me so wonderfully complex! Your workmanship is marvelous — how well I know it."

Live out your faith as an example for your child of your own Christian identity. One mistake I believe parents make is to not let our children know that we have our tough times, too. Be authentic about your own struggles and victories, showing them how to live out their identity in Christ in everyday life. Despite the hardships, let your children know that God is on the throne and that He is a good God!

Encourage and affirm their worth and identity in Jesus every day. Sometimes we get frustrated with our day, and if you are not careful, your bad day can roll off onto your kids. Be sure to always let them know, "You are loved by God, and I love you, too." "God is proud of you, and I am too," or "You are chosen and accepted just as you are." Help build their confidence and self-worth because the world we live in will tear it down by default.

Watching our daughters face peer pressure was something that we as parents kept a constant eye on in their formidable years. Whoever our daughters were around could have a positive impact or a negative impact on them for how they saw themselves, especially as knowing they were daughters of the most high God!

Equip your child through constant encouragement to stand firm in their identity despite societal pressures. Sometimes our daughters would tell us how their peers could be manipulative and mean to say the least. We never gave them the okay to respond in how they were being treated. They were always to act in a Christian manner and not allow anyone to make them think any less of themselves. This is why our church life was so important to us as a family so they would have opportunities to live out their identity in Jesus serving others with their gifts and talents for God's kingdom. Remember, keeping our children in the right environment can build their confidence in their identity in Christ and who He made them to become!

One of the last pictures taken together as a family before our daughters began wanting their boyfriends to become their husbands one by one!

Developing a Biblical Worldview

Shanda and I tried to teach all three of our girls to look for the best in all things, but all things had to be run through the lens of this verse...

Philippians 4:8 (NLT) "And now, dear brothers and sisters, one final thing. Fix your thoughts on what is true, and honorable, and right, and pure, and lovely, and admirable. Think about things that are excellent and worthy of praise."

Teaching our kids discernment helps them to see through what is not good when they fix their thoughts on what is true, honorable and right and pure, and lovely, and admirable. Help your child develop the ability to discern between truth and lies, good and evil. We would discuss different ideologies taking place in media outlets. What does the Bible say, not what the cultural message is. No matter what was taking place in society, everything was looked at from a biblical perspective helping them to see through the lens of God's Word.

As parents, we would tell our daughters not to take anyone's word for what they were hearing and seeing. We would teach them to think for themselves. Do not be gullible, but to think critically about the world around them. Use questions like, "What does the Bible say about this?" challenging them to analyze information and form a biblical worldview.

Not only teach your children to view everything from a biblical perspective but to understand that they are living on mission each day of their life. Help them understand their purpose in the world. Teach them to view their school, friendships, and hobbies as mission fields where they can live out their faith and influence others for Christ.

Shanda and I would tell our daughters to never live in a way that you would compromise your identity and faith in Christ. We taught them that they can be a thermostat or a thermometer. A thermostat changes its atmosphere whereas a thermometer adjusts to the atmosphere. So, we taught them to be a thermostat. Be an example of Christ and demonstrate how to engage with culture without compromising biblical values.

Share how you interact with societal issues, showing a balance between truth and grace, such as addressing cultural challenges with wisdom and compassion. When it came to allowing our daughters to spend the night with one of their friends, if we were aware that their friends' parents did not hold the biblical Christian values that we held, we would not let them spend the night. This could appear to be judgmental, however, this is our children. We would not put them in a position where they could be tempted to compromise their faith through what they would see, hear, or be around. Their friends were always welcome to come to our home to spend the night, though.

One of our daughters wanted to go to a friend's house to spend the night on a particular occasion. Shanda and I did our due diligence about knowing who and where they would be spending the night. Later in the evening, we received a phone call from our daughter that someone there was drinking alcohol openly and acting off, to which our daughter had not been around. This was not our household standard, especially adults doing this around our children. She wanted to come home. When you disciple your children through the lens of the Philippians 4:8 principle, they will own the biblical value for themselves to evaluate all circumstances they are in.

So, encourage a love for God's Word which is the source of their identity and worldview. You and your family may develop a life verse to evaluate all of life circumstances like we did with Philippians 4:8. A life verse serves as a spiritual anchor, helping to filter decisions, attitudes, and responses through the truth of God's Word. When challenges arise, you can return to this verse as a reminder of how God calls us to think and live.

The Bible is not just a book of stories or moral lessons; it is the living, breathing Word of God that shapes our beliefs, values, and actions. When we prioritize Scripture in our homes, we help our children develop a Christ-centered worldview rather than being influenced by the shifting standards of culture.

By making God's Word central in your home, you are equipping your family to stand firm in their faith, develop strong moral convictions, and navigate life's challenges with wisdom and confidence. More than just a habit, Scripture should become a cherished part of your family's culture. Let it shape hearts, strengthens relationships, and deepens their love for Christ.

Reflection Questions:

1. How can you strengthen your child's understanding of their identity in Christ?

2. What steps can you take to affirm your child's worth and God-given identity on a daily basis?

3. How can you help your child navigate the challenges of peer pressure and societal expectations?

A thought to remember...

Empowering our children with a biblical identity is one of the most significant gifts we can give them. It prepares them to face the world with confidence and faith, grounded in the knowledge that they are God's beloved children. Teach them to be a thermostat instead of a thermometer to change the world around them wherever they go to influence others for Christ. When they live in Christ and grow in Christ, their confidence in who they are in Christ will influence those around them.

And as they grow into young adults, may they carry this identity as a beacon of hope, purpose, and strength, impacting the world for Christ's glory.

Chapter 10

Nurturing a Passion for God's Word

Psalm 119:105 (NLT) "Your word is a lamp to guide my feet and a light for my path."

"Children don't need to be told to try harder, believe more, or do better. They need to know that they are loved, that they are rescued, and that God's Word is a story of His never-stopping, never-giving-up, unbreaking, always and forever love."

Sally Lloyd-Jones: author of The Jesus Storybook Bible

Though Shanda and I were Christians when we got married, we were proactive about God's Word. We fell in love with God's Word as we began reading it daily after we married. We read it together and individually. We discovered it was the very heart of God, and it was His main avenue to speak to us. We found out how vital the role of scripture would be for our spiritual formation. We wanted this as well for our daughters when they each came into the world. We didn't say you must read God's Word as a directive as they grew; they saw that it was a daily part of dad and mom's life. It will always be through our example of what we give our time, love, and devotion to that will get the attention of our children especially in their formable years. What we found in parenting in their young years, there was a likelihood that our daughters would love much of what we loved and despise much of what we despised. They did not like my hot peppers to eat for sure, but you get the picture.

A passion for God's Word is foundational to raising spiritually healthy children. The Bible is not just a book of rules and stories; it is a living guide that reveals God's heart and purpose for our lives. Instilling a love for Scripture in our children equips them to make wise decisions, find comfort in trials, and grow closer to God. It is through the Scriptures that they come to understand who God is, what He has done, and what He promises for the future.

Teaching our children to engage with the Bible deeply and meaningfully is a powerful way to shape their faith. A passion for God's Word helps them develop a strong biblical worldview, grow in wisdom, and cultivate a personal relationship with God. It also prepares them to face the challenges of life with confidence and hope.

Benefits of Nurturing a Passion for Scripture

Shanda and I knew that giving our daughters guidance and wisdom would come from God's Word. But it was more so when they were not in our home and out in the world that is not on our side. The Bible provides wisdom for every area of life. Two of my favorite life verses that we taught them was from Proverbs…

Proverbs 3:5-6 (NLT) "Trust in the LORD with all your heart; do not depend on your own understanding.[6] Seek his will in all you do, and he will show you which path to take."

Show your children how God's Word guides decision-making and life choices. Share with them the tough times you face as their parents that you receive strength in times of trials. Give them examples of how scripture offers comfort, encouragement, and hope in difficult times that we all face. Sharing with your children Psalms of comfort, such as Psalm 23 when you and your family go through a hardship…

Psalm 23:1-5 (NLT) "The LORD is my shepherd; I have all that I need.² He lets me rest in green meadows; he leads me beside peaceful streams.³ He renews my strength. He guides me along right paths, bringing honor to his name.⁴ Even when I walk through the darkest valley, I will not be afraid, for you are close beside me. Your rod and your staff protect and comfort me."

Show them how God's Word can be a source of peace in the midst of challenges. Show your children that you have a foundation of faith in God and His Word no matter how turbulent times may get. The deeper our understanding of Scripture is, the more it will strengthen their faith.

Teach them the basics of the Gospel through passages like John 3:16-17, reinforcing the message of salvation. And yes, I did say the 17th verse as well because it is through Jesus Christ that the world can be saved.

John 3:16-17 (NLT) "For this is how God loved the world: He gave his one and only Son, so that everyone who believes in him will not perish but have eternal life. ¹⁷ God sent his Son into the world not to judge the world, but to save the world through him."

Teach your children that reading God's Word is not just downloading information, but it is for their personal transformation. The Word of God has the power to transform hearts and minds. A great transformation example in the Bible to discuss with your children is in Hebrews 4:12.

Hebrews 4:12 (NLT) "For the word of God is alive and powerful. It is sharper than the sharpest two-edged sword, cutting between soul and spirit, between joint and marrow. It exposes our innermost thoughts and desires."

This verse shows the power of Scripture to bring about change in their lives. Reading God's Word is not just looking at lifeless words on paper. The Word of God is alive and powerful. You may not be familiar with why I would say this. In the Gospel of John, the first five verses tell us that God is the Word in Christ Jesus...

John 1:1-5 (NLT) "In the beginning the Word already existed. The Word was with God, and the Word was God.[2] He existed in the beginning with God.[3] God created everything through him, and nothing was created except through him.[4] The Word gave life to everything that was created, and his life brought light to everyone.[5] The light shines in the darkness, and the darkness can never extinguish it."

Jesus Christ is the Word of God who came and dwelt among mankind as the Son of God and as a human man. He was tempted in all the ways we are tempted, yet He never sinned. He willingly went to the cross to fulfill His Father's will to shed His sinless blood for our sinfulness. The same power that brought Jesus back to life on the third day is the same power that we can have to live a victorious life in Him. So, when you need a word for what you or your kids are facing in life, go to the Word of Life! God's Word will be the help we and our children need to be prepared for spiritual warfare. The Scriptures equip them for the spiritual battles they will face. Emphasize to your children this verse in Ephesians 6…

Ephesians 6:17 (NLT) "Put on salvation as your helmet, and take the sword of the Spirit, which is the word of God."

Teaching your children the importance of Scripture as part of their spiritual armor will help them fight the battles that they will undoubtably face in their lives giving them what they need for their future.

Practical Ways to Nurture a Passion for Scripture

Making Scripture accessible and engaging should be a top priority as much as providing them food to eat. Be sure to purchase them Bibles that are age-appropriate and relatable. Do this as soon as you help them to start reading. There are great children's Bibles with simple stories to begin getting them acquainted with God's Word. You can get very creative Bibles that make the stories exciting and fun to read with pictures and illustrations. As your children grow into avid readers, be sure to choose a translation that is easy to understand, such as New Living Translation or the New International Version.

Creating a daily Bible reading routine is vital. You can start with a short passage and simple questions to help them engage with the text. If you haven't started already, incorporate family devotions where you read and discuss the Bible together. This will provide the space for some natural discussion to flow. During this time, encourage your children to memorize key verses and passages that align with your family's faith journey. Celebrate when your children learn a verse of Scripture. My favorite mother-in-law (well, my only mother-in-law), Barbara, known as Mammy to our daughters, challenged all three of them to memorize the 23rd chapter of Psalm. She told them that she would give them twenty dollars each if they could quote it word for word, and they willingly accomplished it! I believe to this day they can still quote it along with much more of God's Word.

Now, I am not saying to pay your kids to learn Scripture, but I am saying to give them incentives. If we, as parents, will give them incentives for good grades, scoring baskets, or touch downs, why would we not give them incentives to know the heart of God?

Here is a great verse to memorize and focus on...

Joshua 1:8 (NLT) "Study this Book of Instruction continually. Meditate on it day and night so you will be sure to obey everything written in it. Only then will you prosper and succeed in all you do."

Helping your children internalize God's Word will be such an amazing help during whatever they face externally in their lives as they grow into future adults. It is vital, though, that you model a love for Scripture as you parent your children. Let them see you engaging with the Bible. Share how God speaks to you through His Word discussing your own Bible study and prayer time with them. Make Scripture a living, active part of your family life. As I touched on earlier, use interactive and fun Bible activities to engage their creativity and involve Scripture, thus helping them to relate to the biblical characters and stories.

Teach your children to apply Scripture in everyday situations. Discuss how a Bible story can relate to something they are experiencing, such as a problem at school, and how God's Word provides wisdom and guidance. When they feel that they cannot accomplish a task, complete a difficult school assignment, or they fear that they will flunk a test, teach them to memorize Philippians 4:13 that I shared earlier. Have them recite it, *"For I can - do everything - through Christ - who gives me strength."* Celebrate with your children a special treat or family outing as a way of affirming their engagement with the Bible.

Creating a Bible-Centered Family Culture

Integrating what you have read in the Bible is a great way to make Scripture part of daily conversations. Talk about Bible stories and scriptures at mealtime, during car rides, or before bedtime prayers, helping them see God's presence in all aspects of life. As parents, we enjoyed a time in our family Bible study where each person shares what they learned that week.

I will never forget the time that my favorite study Bible went missing. I looked everywhere for it. I was sure it was where I had always kept it and couldn't understand what happened with it. After asking my wife and our daughters, our middle daughter India sheepishly divulged to me that she had it. India admitted to her mother and me that she had not been where she needed to be with the Lord and walking with Him. She knew where I kept my Bible, so India got it and started reading it. India realized that she did not have a deep enough heartfelt salvation experience when she was five years old and had come to understand that her first response toward salvation was mostly from her mind decision. Reading God's Word and praying brought her under a state of Holy Spirit conviction. On a trip back from Missouri from seeing our pastor friends, she asked Jesus to forgive her of her sins and was born again! I could have never been more joyful that India got my Bible and began to read the heart of God which led her to true salvation in Jesus Christ!

Shanda and I were intentional about having our family devotion times that helped develop a passion for understanding God's truth. We would focus on biblical characters or doctrinal truths, helping them connect those teachings to their own life. Shanda and I give all the glory to God that we tried to consistently model our personal faithfulness to God's Word, our prayer life, and putting it into practice. It set an example which led India to her own heartfelt salvation. I cannot emphasize enough as parents that you demonstrate faithfulness in living out Scripture. Live out biblical principles in your daily life, such as honesty, kindness, forgiveness, and love, showing them how these values are lived out in the real world.

Reflection Questions:

1. How can you help your child develop a love for God's Word?

2. What are some ways you can integrate Bible reading into your family's daily routine?

3. How can you model a passion for Scripture in your own life?

A thought to remember...

Nurturing a passion for God's Word is one of the greatest gifts you can give your child. When they learn to love and treasure Scripture, they will have a source of wisdom, guidance, and strength that will serve them well throughout their lives. There will never be a greater source of wisdom than God's Word for the future adults you are raising to lean on in this world that we live in.

As your children grow, may God's Word illuminate their path, helping them to walk in truth, grace, and love. May your family's journey be marked by these values, leading to a deeper faith and a more meaningful relationship with God. Our children are God's before they ever were ours, so helping them with an all-out love for His heart which is God's Word will be the lifeline in every part of their lives.

Chapter 11

Parenting Prodigal Kids

Isaiah 49:15-16a (NLT) "Never! Can a mother forget her nursing child? Can she feel no love for the child she has borne? But even if that were possible, I would not forget you! 16 See, I have written your name on the palms of my hands."

"You may have strayed from the path, but God's love will always guide you home." Billy Graham

When it comes to knowing first-hand about parenting a prodigal child, I write this chapter from being the prodigal child. When I look back on what I put my parents through, I see the love they portrayed for me, their hearts of being Christians, and applying the Biblical principles I will share. I regret to this day what I put my parents through. However, because of their unceasing love for me, the many prayers they lifted to the Lord on my behalf, and through patience, they witnessed God turn a dope dealer into a hope dealer. I wonder if they complained to the Lord when each of them went to Heaven for all I put them through? After all, you don't get the nickname "Terrible Terrell" for nothing.

Parenting often begins with an overwhelming sense of hope and wonder. When parents hold their newborn for the first time, they're captivated by the tiny, innocent life entrusted to them. While the baby may not resemble an angel (perhaps more like a mix of Papa Smurf and E.T.), parents are quick to declare, "My baby is perfect." But the reality is more complex. Every child is born with a sin nature—a universal truth underscored in the Bible and found in Romans 3…

Romans 3:10-12 (NLT) "As the Scriptures say, "No one is righteous not even one.[11] No one is truly wise; no one is seeking God.[12] All have turned away; all have become useless. No one does good, not a single one."

This is not to discourage parents but to prepare them for the journey ahead. When children are small, parents dream of their potential and envision bright futures. But no parent imagines their child growing up to rebel, backtalk, or fall into destructive behaviors. Despite even the best intentions, there are moments when children stray from their upbringing, becoming prodigals. I was the prodigal for my parents, and I regret the pain that I caused them from my waywardness, disrespect, disobedience, and thinking, "I know it all."

Understanding the Prodigal Path

The term "prodigal" refers to someone who wastes their resources or purpose through riotous, reckless living. It's a painful reality for many parents as children sometimes choose a path far removed from the one their parents envisioned. Yet, this heartbreak is not unfamiliar to God.

Isaiah 1:2-3 (NLT) "Listen O heavens! Pay attention, earth! This is what the Lord says: "The children I raised and cared for have rebellion against me. [3] Even an ox knows its owner, and a donkey recognizes its master's care- but Israel doesn't know its master. My people don't recognize my care for them."

As Isaiah 1:2-3 illustrates, even God's children—Israel—turned away despite His care. If you've ever wondered why your child abandoned your values, remember that God Himself understands your pain. The parable of the prodigal son (Luke 15:11-32) offers profound insight into this experience. The story is a vivid picture of self-centeredness, rebellion, and the eventual journey home. Let's unpack this story to better understand how to parent prodigals.

The Prodigal's Pride

Luke 15:11-13a (NLT) "To illustrate the point further, Jesus told them this story: "A man had two sons. 12 The younger son told his father, 'I want my share of your estate now before you die.' So his father agreed to divide his wealth between his sons. 13 "A few days later this younger son packed all his belongings and moved to a distant land,"

The younger son's demand for his inheritance—essentially wishing his father were dead—reveals the hallmarks of a prodigal heart: self-centeredness, arrogance, and impatience. Prodigals become consumed with their own desires, convinced they know best. Parents often experience this firsthand when a child hits adolescence, suddenly dismissing parental wisdom. Like the prodigal son, these individuals pursue immediate gratification, throwing caution to the wind.

Luke 13b-16 (NLT) "and there he wasted all his money in wild living. 14 About the time his money ran out, a great famine swept over the land, and he began to starve. 15 He persuaded a local farmer to hire him, and the man sent him into his fields to feed the pigs. 16 The young man became so hungry that even the pods he was feeding the pigs looked good to him. But no one gave him anything."

Luke 15:13b-16 paints a vivid picture of his descent — wasting his inheritance on wild living, only to end up feeding pigs, a task unthinkable for a Jewish man. Sin's allure often leads to rock bottom, a place where many prodigals eventually find themselves. From what I went through in my prodigal years, it took me hitting rock bottom and getting, "Sick and tired of being sick and tired."

When Parenting a Prodigal Hurts

Watching a child go astray can be devastating. Parents often spiral into self-blame, questioning every decision: "Did we spoil them too much?" "Should we have been stricter?" "What if we had sent them to private school?" While introspection can be valuable, it's important to remember that parents are not solely responsible for their children's choices. Just as parents cannot take full credit for their child's successes, they cannot bear full blame for their struggles. Ultimately, everyone is accountable to God.

Reaching Prodigals

So, what can parents do when their child becomes a prodigal? I want to share three principles that can offer guidance to you to give you direction and hope for those who may have strayed away like I did. With God's help, you can see them get on the right path for His purpose and for your peace of heart and mind.

Never Stop Praying

Prayer is the most powerful tool parents have. Praying to the God, who spoke this universe into existence and knit us all together in our mother's womb, loves hearing from His children when we are in pain about the children He gave us! Read these two verses...

Colossians 1:9-10 (NLT) "So we have not stopped praying for you since we first heard about you. We ask God to give you complete knowledge of his will and to give you spiritual wisdom and understanding. ¹⁰ Then the way you live will always honor and please the Lord, and your lives will produce every kind of good fruit. All the while, you will grow as you learn to know God better and better."

Colossians 1:9-10 reminds us of the transformative power of intercession: "We have not stopped praying for you..." Parents may feel they've tried everything—discipline, counseling, grounding—to no avail. But prayer should always be the first line of defense. Through prayer, parents can ask God to remove harmful influences from their child's life. Friends, environments, or habits that encourage rebellion or sin can be powerful stumbling blocks for a prodigal. Parents should pray that God would distance their child from these influences, even if it means painful separations. Trust that removing toxic influences creates space for healing and growth. Bring the right friends into their path.

Prodigals often surround themselves with peers who reinforce destructive choices. I know this from personal experience that not only caused myself much heartache but caused my parents' undue pain. Parents can intercede for Godly, positive friendships that will inspire their child toward better decisions. A single positive relationship can be transformative, leading a prodigal back to truth. Allow consequences to lead the prodigal toward repentance.

Consequences are often the turning point in a prodigal son's story.

While it's natural for parents to want to shield their child from pain, allowing them to face the results of their actions can be a powerful teacher. Pray for strength to let natural consequences occur, trusting and hoping that these moments can bring clarity and humility to a prodigal's heart. Pray persistently and passionately, trusting God to work in ways unseen.

Practice Never-Ending Patience

Read what Galatians 6:9 urges about enduring...

Galatians 6:9 (NLT) "So let's not get tired of doing what is good. At just the right time we will reap a harvest of blessing if we don't give up."

Parenting a prodigal requires incredible patience. The father in the parable likely scanned the horizon daily, hoping for his son's return. Parents of prodigals must embody that same relentless hope, refusing to give up. I want you to soak in 2 Timothy 2:24 from The Passion translation ...

2 Timothy 2:24 (TPT) "For a true servant of our Lord Jesus will not be argumentative but gentle toward all and skilled in helping others see the truth, having great patience toward the immature."

We are to not to be argumentative as servants of Jesus Christ, and here, it furthermore calls for gentleness and patience toward the immature. Even when prodigals are stubborn, patience plants seeds for future growth. I distinctly remember my parents trying to reason with me when I was out of God's will in how I was living. Our conversations always would end up in an argument because I thought I knew so much more than what they knew.

In my particular situation, I had to get to the bottom of the smelly hog pen and come to my senses...

Luke 15:17-19 (NLT) "When he finally came to his senses, he said to himself, 'At home even the hired servants have food enough to spare, and here I am dying of hunger! [18] *I will go home to my father and say, "Father, I have sinned against both heaven and you,* [19] *and I am no longer worthy of being called your son. Please take me on as a hired servant."'*

Don't ever give up praying for your prodigal son or daughter. My parents and my grandmother did not give up on praying for me. I was on my prodigal journey about 12 years. I suggest that you pray for them to come to their senses and for God to keep them safe wherever their prodigal journey exists until God brings them home.

Luke 15:20a (NLT) "So he returned home to his father. And while he was still a long way off, his father saw him coming."

I wonder if the son's father looked multiple times a day for his son to come home and thought, "Maybe today will be the day that my son will come home."

Demonstrate Unconditional Love

Every time I read this story, I think and try to imagine the father's look in his eyes when he saw his son in the distance. If I could have been there to see what his eyes looked like, I believe that whatever pain was once in them now was dispelled with tears of such love and joy. The father's response to his returning son in Luke 15:20 is nothing short of extraordinary.

Luke 15:20 (NLT) "So he returned home to his father. And while he was still a long way off, his father saw him coming. Filled with love and compassion, he ran to his son, embraced him, and kissed him."

Filled with compassion, he ran to his son, embraced him, and celebrated his return. This love was not contingent on the son's behavior but rooted in grace. In Jewish culture, running—especially for an older man—was considered undignified. Yet the father ran to protect his son from the scorn of the villagers. He clothed him in a robe, placed a ring on his finger, and threw a feast. This extravagant love mirrors God's love for us, a love that welcomes sinners home.

The Bigger Picture

Ultimately, the story of the prodigal son is about more than parenting. It's a reflection of God's grace. Every one of us has, at some point, been a prodigal—self-centered, rebellious, and in need of redemption. Yet, God waits for us with open arms ready to celebrate our return.

Isaiah 30:18a (NLT) declares, "So the LORD must wait for you to come to him so he can show you his love and compassion."

Whether you're a parent of a prodigal or a prodigal yourself, know this: God's love never fails, and His grace is always sufficient.

Reflection Questions

1. How does understanding that even God's children (Israel) rebelled against Him change your perspective on parenting a prodigal?

2. What does the parable of the prodigal son teach you about patience and unconditional love in parenting?

3. In what ways can you demonstrate both prayerful surrender and persistent hope for a prodigal in your life?

A thought to remember...

As you reflect on this chapter, think of the prodigal in your life. No parent dreams of raising a prodigal, but every prodigal is still a beloved child. Whether you are waiting for a wayward child to return or you yourself have walked that road, the story of the prodigal son is a testimony of God's unchanging love. His grace is greater than rebellion, and His patience outlasts our wandering. Lift their name in prayer, ask God for patience, and commit to showing them unconditional love. Keep praying, keep hoping, and trust that God's love is strong enough to bring the lost home. If you're the prodigal, remember that God is waiting with open arms. No matter how far you've strayed, His grace is enough to bring you home.

Chapter 12

Parents Passing Christian Heritage

Psalm 78:4 (NLT) "We will not hide these truths from our children; we will tell the next generation about the glorious deeds of the Lord, about His power and His mighty wonders."

"If we don't teach our children who God is, someone else will teach them everything that He isn't." R.C. Sproul

One of the richest gifts parents can give their children is a living Christian heritage, a legacy worth passing on. It is all about sharing a faith story that predates the children's birth that will endure long after they reach adulthood. This heritage is about more than church attendance or a collection of beliefs; it is a tapestry woven from stories of God's faithfulness, family traditions rooted in Scripture, and personal testimonies of how the gospel shapes daily life.

When parents consistently speak of God's works in the past, point to His hand in the present, and hope in His promises for the future, they create a legacy that young hearts can embrace, cherish, and ultimately pass on to the generations that follow.

The Biblical basis for passing down faith to your children is to remember God's mighty acts throughout Scripture.

God's people were commanded to remember and retell God's works…

Deuteronomy 4:9 (NLT) "But watch out! Be careful never to forget what you yourself have seen. Do not let these memories escape from your mind as long as you live! And be sure to pass them on to your children and grandchildren."

These stories of deliverance, provision, and guidance strengthen faith and anchor future generations in God's character. Teach the next generation like the psalmist, calling God's people to tell the coming generation the glorious deeds of the Lord (Psalm 78:4). By recounting stories of salvation and ongoing testimonies of God's goodness, parents fulfill this divine instruction.

Leading our children by example comes through modeling love for God. Deuteronomy 6:5-7 gives instructions of how to pass faith to our children…

*Deuteronomy 6:5-7 (NLT) "And you must love the L*ORD *your God with all your heart, all your soul, and all your strength. ⁶ And you must commit yourselves wholeheartedly to these commands that I am giving you today. ⁷ Repeat them again and again to your children. Talk about them when you are at home and when you are on the road, when you are going to bed and when you are getting up."*

These verses remind parents to love the Lord wholeheartedly and to diligently pass that devotion to their children. The daily rhythms of life, mealtimes, walking together, and bedtime routines become sacred opportunities for imparting a Christian heritage. Our three daughters have written the following pages of how being raised in a Christian home has impacted how Christ is the center of their family's lives for passing faith to their children.

Our oldest daughter Lily Freeman shares...

I know that growing up in a Christian household looks different for everyone. Of course, there are probably, and hopefully biblical principles taught, prayers said at mealtimes, and morals in place that look different from the world we live in. Growing up in a pastor's home is one of the many blessings of this life the Lord has given me that I hold most dear to my heart. As the oldest, I got to experience all the "firsts" through trial and error. I tried to be the best role model I could for my little sisters, while learning to follow the ways of the Lord as I grew in Him, with our parents guiding. Church wasn't just a place we went; it was our way of life.

A normal morning waking up in the Somerville household looked like tip toeing down the stairs into the kitchen and living room while the coffee was brewing. I would see my dad with his head bowed down praying in quiet murmurs. I would hear the rustling of pages in his Bible. We knew to not make a peep, because this time was the most important and holy part of his day, meeting with the Lord.

My mom would either be in the kitchen preparing breakfast and helping get us girls ready, or she would be sitting down doing a devotional being with the Lord in the early daylight as well. Then, before we would head off on the school bus, whether we were running late or not as three young girls do, Dad would always read a short scripture when time allowed. No one could leave until we joined hands and prayed together before we went our separate ways for the day.

I remember my mama singing worship songs in the car or sitting at the piano to play "Trust and Obey", which I now sing to my own children. All of these moments were practices woven into our daily life, but now as I look back on it as a woman of thirty-three with my own children, I treasure these moments deeply. They have profoundly shaped my personal faith in the Lord and how my husband and I help steward our children's faith as they begin and continue their journeys with Jesus.

My parents took Joshua 24:15 seriously...

"But as for me and my family, we will serve the LORD."

Why? Because no matter what obstacles would come our way, as for our house, we were serving the Lord. Our story as a family is unique in the way that no matter where the Lord called my dad to lead, he would go. We spent our time at various churches as God would lead him to preach and carry His message. Because of that, we got to meet and connect with people from all different walks of life.

As pastor's kids, we attended many functions that other "regular church kids" probably didn't, like funerals. Imagine walking in a funeral home with many people you don't know, and the smell of fried chicken wafting through the air. At least 40 to 50 people are mourning their lost loved one in the room while saying things like, "They look good, don't they?" The room filled with the putrid fragrance of carnations while I clung to my Daddy's leg because I was actually quite terrified of being in the room with a dead person. In the south where we grew up, funerals weren't just to commemorate someone close to you who has passed, they were a social gathering. And for a pastor's kid, well, it was just a normal Thursday afternoon.

We were no stranger to deep, theological discussions about salvation, death, where we would spend eternity, and when Christ would return. Moreover, now when I look back on those deep discussions that were never sugarcoated but full of God's truth and grace, I am beyond grateful. Growing up as a pastor's kid often felt like living under a microscope because you were held to a higher standard. I often felt the pressure of that but did the best I knew how to lead a life that looked like Jesus to the world.

Other kids might have not had those conversations, but because we did, I really believe that, although in my life I have strayed and fallen short of God's glory, I have always taken my relationship with the Lord seriously. Because of my mother worshipping in the car, I have a passion for making worship a daily part of my life.

Being in the room many times with those who have lost loved ones, I have been able to sit with others in their grief, all the while learning to cling closer to Jesus when walking through my own. Because we talked about eternity and Jesus coming back one day, I take the gospel and preparing my heart for His return seriously. I have developed a deep fear of the Lord and hope for eternity that I want to share with my children and others. In these unique experiences, I have been able to find the sweetest joy in the deepest sorrow.

I have always wanted to walk with Jesus closely and intimately, like He is my best friend right beside me, because He is. I feel the longing in my heart to obey His commands and trust Him with my whole heart leaning not on my own understanding (Proverbs 3:5). I believe that He is working all things together for the good of those who love Him and are called according to His purpose (Romans 8:28) because of my loving parents. They weren't always perfect, but who is? It is through the perfect image of Jesus that they trained us in the way we should go, knowing that because of their faith, hope, and love for Jesus Christ and their children, that we would not depart from it. It is because of that faith, hope, and love that our children and future generations ahead will have an opportunity to truly know Him.

Our middle daughter India Goostree tells...

I could start my experience of Spiritually Freed Parenting by focusing on my raising in a "Christian" home, but that would be severely understating the reality. I did not just grow up in a "Christian" home, I grew up in a Christ-centered home. There is a difference. All across America, a multitude of parents claim to be Christian parents. They attend church a couple of times a year or maybe a couple of times a month. But often, there is a severe disconnect between the teachings of the church and the culture of their home. I say this with no condemnation, but with deep grief, concern, and love.

My core memories as a child are rooted in two primary environments: my family member's homes and the rows of churches. All of my life, I have been planted in the church. I don't remember a time where faith was not the determining factor of everything in my family's life. Our schedules were centered on the church calendar, and our lives intertwined with church members. The culture of our home and the culture of our church were almost transcendent. My parents were imperfect. We knew that, our church knew that, and our community knew that. Yet, they were Christ-centered. That made all the difference.

The reality of being a pastor's kid was both beautiful and brutal. We saw weddings and funerals, tragedies and triumphs, wins and losses. We often gained friends, only to see our relationships uprooted by church division. We watched our parents be honored and hated, respected and vilified. These are often the shared experiences of the pastor's children. Sadly, however, not all pastors' children live in Christ-centered homes. The difference is whether or not they live what they preach. For the most part, my parents did. When they failed, they expressed true repentance. We knew in spite of their flaws; they loved God, and they loved us.

Being a Pastor's kid came with its unique share of experiences, yet the foundation of faith we received can be applicable to every parent and not exclusive to solely children in pastor's families. I believe every single parent has a call and responsibility to discipline their children in the faith, and that begins by making Christ the center of everything.

Since becoming a mother myself, I recognize that curating a Christ-centered home is a daunting task. In fact, in some ways, it feels impossible. But as Matthew 19:26 (NIV) says, *"With God all things are possible."* I have four children: Karlee (21), Zion (5), Isaac (3) and Silas (2 months.) I have had to implement many changes in my life in order to consistently keep God at the center of our family. Christ-centered parenting comes with a great cost, and following Jesus will cost you everything. Jesus said...

Matthew 16:25 (NIV) *"For whoever wants to save his life will lose it, but whoever loses their life for Me will find it."*

In 2019, my son Zion was born. I discovered my pregnancy in our church hallway when a church brother came and prophesied over me that I was pregnant with a boy. Before I even knew I was a mother, the Holy Spirit was inviting me to co-parent with Him. A pregnancy test did not reveal my motherhood, the Holy Spirit did! Nine months later, I birthed my first son.

Shortly after my son Zion's birth, I chose to resign from full time vocational ministry in my church and make more room for time with my new child. This was one of the hardest and most rewarding decisions of my life. It cost us a portion of our income yet gave us the gift of time to hear from God about where He was leading our family. His plans were so much greater and different than our own.

In the years to follow, God called us to continue to lay down our lives to raise our children. When my son Isaac was due, I resigned from a part-time position I had taken to give my full attention to Him. I not only resigned from that job, but we shortly after sold our dream home due to the financial effects of me being a new stay-at-home mother.

Shortly before Isaac's birth, we felt led to open our home to foster or adopt. Within a couple weeks of starting foster classes, I listened to a podcast called "An Unusual Adoption Story" where a couple our age with children the same ages as our biological children were called to adopt a girl that God placed in their path. I wept as I listened to their faith to bring a full-grown teen into their home and adopt her after she had come of age. That very night after listening to that podcast, a college-aged student from my husband's youth group informed us that she would soon be homeless. Her history was riddled with pain, loss, and instability. She needed a home, but more than that, she needed love.

As she shared her story with me, I remembered the podcast from that morning. I remembered how I felt the Spirit of God bear witness in my soul that He loved His dear children who do not have families, regardless of their age. Psalm 68:6 states that *"God places the lonely in families."* I realized immediately that God was calling us to let Karlee not only live in our home but be a member of our family.

Six months later, on her 19th birthday, Karlee became a permanent member of our family. The same spirit that spoke in advance the birth of each of my sons by Bible verses, prophecies, and dreams, also spoke in advance the adoption of our daughter. Henry Blackaby states in his study *Experiencing God* that *"God speaks by the Holy Spirit through the bible, prayer, circumstances, and the church to reveal Himself, His purposes, and His ways."* Through Christ-centered parenting, we can experience God in profound ways that are peculiar to the world.

The primary difference between Christian parents and Christ-centered parents is prioritizing obedience to the voice of God at all costs. Parents who are willing to pay any price to obey the voice of God will inevitably model a functional faith with their actions, not just their words.

Parenting will not just be a Sunday sermon, but a Monday ministry.

God promises to speak to us and guide us in this life. We often are tempted to harden our hearts when the cost of following God seems to be too much. But it is only through obedience that we can live spiritually freed lives and be spiritually freed parents.

Spiritually Freed Parenting requires us to be sensitive to the presence of God. I often do not know the next step to take as a mother, but God does. We must consult the Spirit of God in every area, and especially in parenting. Our parenthood must be fueled by prayer, guided by scripture, and submitted to the Lordship of Jesus. We are not called to be perfect parents, but we are called to be obedient parents. Every spiritually freed parent must first be parented by God Himself. This is the key to spirit-led parenting.

Our youngest daughter Chloe Pedigo recalls...

"Rise and shine, and give God the glory, glory! Rise and shine, and give God the glory, glory! Rise and shine, and give God the glory, glory, children of the Lord!" Growing up, that was often the song we awoke to with our mother singing as she turned on our bedroom lights. We would all make our way to the kitchen and quietly go about as our dad was finishing his devotion and prayer time in his red recliner. When it was time to part ways, my dad would typically take me to my grade school, and my mom would take my sisters to their schools. Most mornings, we would all gather together in a circle and hold hands while we prayed. Sometimes a "popcorn" prayer, sometimes just one leading, but always sharing the burdens on each of our hearts and taking those to the throne room in some way before we went our separate ways each day.

Amidst varying responsibilities of ministry, planting a church, building houses, part-time jobs, raising a family, and more, my parents certainly juggled a lot. I would be lying if I said it was always sunshine and rainbows, and I know they would say the same! However, I feel so blessed to have been raised in a Christian home with parents who raised us to seek after the Lord above all else.

As I reflect on my childhood, as a whole, the main thing that stands out to me is how my parents made the time and practiced intentional parenting and discipline. If there was a teachable moment to be had, they tried their best to act on it, then and there. If any of us were directly disobedient, we were to recite Colossians 3:20 (KJV)...

"Children, obey your parents in all things, for this is well pleasing unto the Lord."

If any of us were ever complaining too much, we were to name all of the things we were thankful for, one by one. If we were arguing, we would have to say something we loved about one another, then hug "without smiling" which usually resulted in us laughing and forgetting why we were arguing in the first place! My parents have always believed and truly tried to practice that faith starts at home.

As the youngest of three, I always thought there was something so beautiful about the sibling bond and big families in general. I knew that if the good Lord was willing, I wanted to raise a big family myself. As an "old soul" (or so I've been called), I knew the Lord wanted me to stay home and homeschool my kids from when I was in elementary school. I met and started dating my now husband when I was in middle school. I graduated high school early, got married to Jared at eighteen, and now we have five beautiful children together!

They say, with age, you typically grow to respect and understand your parents more. While I think that is true, I think it's true on an entirely different level when you actually become a parent yourself. Since the moment I became a parent, I suddenly had a lot more grace and respect for my parents. I started to see how hard it actually can be, how much weight and heart goes into every little decision, how much each little life means, how much you would do to protect them, and most of all, how desperately you want to raise them to know and love Jesus.

Now that I am a parent myself, I see myself repeating a lot of the same patterns and methods my parents used to raise us. I often find myself singing "rise and shine" to my kids in the morning, praying with them regularly, having them recite what they are thankful for, or practice hugging it out! However "annoying" I found it at times as a kid, the truth is that a lot of these seemingly mundane, day-in and day-out parenting patterns is what helped shape me and my sisters into the women we are today.

While I know not everyone had the privilege of growing up in a stable, safe, Christian household, I am so thankful and honored to have had that example laid out for me. And the beauty of it all is that no matter what your past is or where you may find yourself in your own parenting journey, our

God is a redeemer, and there is hope in Jesus! There are no generational curses or addictions that He can't break, and you could be the very one He is using to change your family tree!

Reflection Questions:

1. What spiritual milestones or celebrations can you establish to mark Gods work in your children's lives?

2. Are there any cultural pressures, family dynamics, or busyness factors hindering your ability to pass on a Christian heritage?

3. How can you encourage your child's curiosity and questions about faith?

A thought to remember…

Passing on a Christian heritage is both a divine calling and a joyful privilege. When you weave Gods faithfulness into your family's ongoing story, you equip your children with a deep sense of belonging and a robust spiritual foundation. Long after your direct influence has waned, and let me say that season flies by, they will carry the torch of faith shining the light of Christ into their own generation and beyond. May God bless your family's legacy, using your faithful testimony to inspire future adults who will continue His story of redemption, hope, and love in the world.

Conclusion

Raising Future Adults God's Way

Raising spiritually healthy and empowered children is one of the greatest responsibilities and privileges we have as parents. In this book, we've explored the essentials of parenting God's way, nurturing their identity in Christ, cultivating a heart of gratitude, fostering a passion for Scripture, and preparing them to live as future adults who are grounded in their faith. These principles lay the foundation for a life that is not only meaningful and fulfilling but also one that reflects the love and character of Christ.

As parents, our primary role is to disciple our children to lead them to a deeper understanding of God's love, to equip them with the tools they need to live out their faith, and to empower them to make a difference in the world. This journey is not without its challenges, but it is one that is filled with incredible rewards. When we raise our children with a biblical worldview, we prepare them not just for the present but for the future, equipping them to face the uncertainties of life with confidence, hope, and faith.

Living out the lessons of "Spiritually FREED Parenting, Raising Future Adults" will have its greatest impact for our children when we lead by example. Shanda and I did not have our parenting down pat but gave our best effort to model a life of faith. Children learn best from what they see. Model a life that reflects your own faith journey. Show them what it means to live out the principles of God's Word in everyday life through your actions, attitudes, and choices. Let them see you pray, read the Bible, and trust God amid trials. By doing so, you will not only teach them about God but also show them the reality of a living, active faith.

Create a Christ-Centered Home where God's presence is felt in every corner in how you relate to each other, in your family routines, and in the decisions you make. Fill your home with reminders of God's love and faithfulness through scripture on the walls, prayers at mealtime, and conversations that point back to biblical truths. In such an environment, your children will learn to see God during their everyday lives.

Empower your children to live their faith. As they grow, provide opportunities for your children to live out their faith in real-world settings. Encourage them to serve, to share their faith, and to take on leadership roles in the church and community. Help them discover and use their spiritual gifts, supporting them as they explore what God has called them to do. Equip them to be the hands and feet of Jesus in the world, ready to make a difference for His kingdom.

Encourage your children to have a lifelong pursuit of God. Living for God is not a sprint, it is a marathon. Life is a journey of continual growth. Encourage your children to seek God daily to read His Word, to pray, and to listen for His voice. Help them develop spiritual disciplines that will serve them well throughout their lives. Teach them to rely on the Holy Spirit for guidance, strength, and wisdom, knowing that God's presence is with them every step of the way.

I want to reiterate that as parents, you celebrate your children's spiritual milestones. As your children grow in their faith, giving them kudos for how you see them become more like Jesus gives them their own sense of accomplishment. It shows them you are proud of them, whether it's the day they give their life to Christ, the day they are baptized, or the day they demonstrate a deeper understanding of God's Word. As your kids continue growing spiritually, step up to serve in their spiritual giftedness, see that all they own is God's while bringing tithes and offerings to church, whatever the ways you see them growing in Jesus, celebrate these moments as significant milestones in their spiritual journey. Let these celebrations be markers of God's faithfulness and the ongoing work He is doing in their lives.

A Final Charge

Raising children who are spiritually healthy and prepared for the future is a journey that requires intentionality, prayer, and reliance on God's wisdom. But it is a journey worth taking. As you apply the principles shared in this book, you are partnering with God in the sacred task of parenting, preparing your children to become future adults who are rooted in faith, confident in their identity, and ready to impact the world for Christ.

I know, as I can speak for Shanda and myself in our parenting journey, we are so thankful that God through His Holy Spirit was always there for us to make up for our mistakes in our parenting journey. We knew God's grace was always sufficient to help us in our deficiencies. God helped us despite of ourselves, and we know that He will help you, too! May God bless you on this journey, giving you wisdom, strength, and joy as you raise the next generation to live spiritually FREED in Jesus Christ!

Prayer for Parents

Heavenly Father, thank You for the gift of parenthood. As we raise our children, help us to be faithful stewards of the responsibility You have given us. Grant us the wisdom and grace to lead them to a deeper understanding of Your love and truth. Fill our homes with Your peace and joy, and blessings. Help us to model a life of faith that inspires our children to follow You wholeheartedly. We surrender our parenting to You, trusting that You will guide us every step of the way. In Jesus' name, Amen.

All our family! It was a feat to get us together with all our grandchildren!

From left to right, Chloe, myself, my wife, Shanda, Lily, & India

Acknowledgements

Thanks, most of all, to my Lord and Savior Jesus Christ who saved my soul from sin and gave me the opportunity to serve Him as a Christian, husband, father, Papa T, and as a pastor. Without Him, I would not be who I am today! I cannot give enough praise and adoration to Jesus for giving me my relationship with Him through the power, guidance, conviction, and leadership of the Holy Spirit.

I am so grateful, humbled, and honored to have my wife Shanda by my side. Without her and all her sacrifices as a wife, mother for our three daughters, and to help hold my arms up to lead our church family, this book would not have been possible. I will never be able to thank God enough for the amazing Motherhood she has shown through her parenting to our daughters and as Nana to our 11 grandchildren and counting!

Shanda and I are so thankful and proud of our three daughters, Lily, India, and Chloe. Thanks be to God that He gave us each of you for the honor, privilege, and responsibility to raise you in His love and ways. Glory to God to see each of you grow up to become the Christian ladies, wives, mothers, and leaders in the faith and to see how you each are passing faith to your children. Thank you for the grace you gave to us because we were far from being perfect parents, but wanted most of all for you to know, intimately, our perfect Heavenly Father through His Son Jesus Christ!

I also want to thank my parents who are now in Heaven, who led me in the ways of Jesus Christ. I am so grateful that they passed faith in Jesus to me through their example. I am thankful to my mother-in-law and father-in-law, Randall and Barbara Prock, who passed faith in Jesus to their daughter Shanda. Together, Shanda and I had the privilege and honor to pass faith in Jesus to our daughters!

I want to thank Allen Sircy for his continued encouragement to inspire me to write and help me with the publishing logistics. I am thankful for Tyler Feller for helping with the graphic cover design and other logistics for printing. Also, I am thankful to Rhonda Vaughn, Chelsie Sircy, and Trudy Conover for taking time to edit the transcript.

This book is dedicated to all of you! Shanda and I pray that you may have found something in these pages that would help you in any way on your parenting journey. I know from our personal parenting journey, we needed all the help we could get! So, may God richly bless you with His wisdom through His presence, power, and Word to raise the gifts of your children God has given you! As Numbers 6:24-26 (NLT) says in the Old Testament, *"May the Lord bless you and protect you. May the Lord smile on you and be gracious to you. May the Lord show you favor and give you His peace."*

Another book available on Amazon by

Terrell Somerville